# Social Policy in the 1990s

## Agenda for Reform

Thomas J. Courchene

*Policy Study No. 3*
*C.D. Howe Institute*

C.D. Howe Institute publications are available from:

Prentice-Hall Canada Inc.
1870 Birchmount Road
Scarborough, Ontario
M1P 2J7
(416) 293-3621

**Canadian Cataloguing in Publication Data**
Courchene, Thomas, J., 1940–
  Social policy in the 1990s

(Policy study, ISSN 0832-7912; no. 3)
Includes bibliographical references.
ISBN 0-88806-138-2

1. Canada – Social policy. I. C.D. Howe Institute.
II. Title. III. Series: Policy study (C.D. Howe Institute); no. 3.

HN107.C68 1987    361.6'1'0971    C87-093757-X

To my parents, Gen and Al, in Wakaw, Saskatchewan

# Contents

# List of Abbreviations

| | |
|---|---|
| BTT | Business transfer tax |
| CAP | Canada Assistance Plan |
| CEC | Canada Employment Centre |
| CPP/QPP | Canada Pension Plan/Quebec Pension Plan |
| DREE | Department of Regional Economic Expansion |
| DRIE | Department of Regional Industrial Expansion |
| GAI | Guaranteed annual income |
| GAINS | Guaranteed Annual Income System |
| GIS | Guaranteed Income Supplement |
| HMO | Health maintenance organization |
| NIT | Negative income tax |
| OAS | Old Age Security |
| OECD | Organisation for Economic Co-operation and Development |
| PIT | Personal income tax |
| RPP | Registered Pension Plan |
| RRSP | Registered Retirement Savings Plan |
| TAAP | Transitional Adjustment Assistance Program |
| UI | Unemployment insurance |
| UISP | Universal Income Security Program |
| VAT | Value-added tax |

# Foreword

Social policy in Canada today is well established as one of the most important responsibilities of government. Federal and provincial social programs expanded dramatically in size and complexity in the 1960s and 1970s, involving more beneficiaries, more taxpayers, much bigger benefits, and a larger slice of the national income. In the 1980s, Canadians have become much more aware of the broad range of their social programs. Together with slower economic growth and large budget deficits, this new awareness has brought about a rethinking of the role of social policy.

This study, by Professor Thomas J. Courchene of the University of Western Ontario and a Senior Fellow of the C.D. Howe Institute, is an important contribution to greater understanding of the entire spectrum of federal and provincial government social programs. Courchene's theme is that Canada's social policy network faces important demographic, fiscal, and economic challenges in the 1990s. Social policy reform must address shifting social and demographic patterns, encourage ongoing restructuring of the economy, and aid the process of rebuilding the fiscal integrity of Canadian governments. The present social policy system, designed to meet the needs of the 1960s, is not up to the task of meeting the challenges of the 1990s.

Courchene argues that, to meet these challenges, Canadians will have to confront three fundamental types of choices or trade-offs. The first is the need to enhance economic security on the one hand and maintain flexibility to respond to a rapidly changing economic environment on the other hand. The second is the trade-off between centralizing responsibility for social policy at the federal level to provide similar benefits and services across the country and decentralizing responsibility to encourage the provinces to be innovative in meeting local needs. The third trade-off is the choice between the provision of social services by the private sector or by the public sector.

In his broad-ranging assessment of Canadian social policy, Courchene divides the system into four components: the retirement income subsystem, the welfare work subsystem, the established programs (health and education) subsystem, and the equalization subsystem. In each case, he diagnoses the strengths and weaknesses of the current system, examines options for reform, and presents his own preferred approach in light of the challenges the system faces. The result is an agenda for reform based on a unique overview of the integrated and interdependent nature of Canada's social policy network.

Courchene concludes that the social policy goals developed over the past 25 years remain every bit as valid as they ever were. Because of changing social and economic factors and the development of new, more preferable social policy instruments, however, reform is now badly needed. The federal government's decision to pursue comprehensive tax reform has greatly expanded the potential for social policy reform, since social benefits increasingly have come to be delivered through the tax system. The opportunity now exists to undertake, in an incremental fashion, a fundamental reorientation of Canadian social policy to meet the social and economic challenges of the 1990s.

New challenges are constantly emerging. Public support for child care very quickly became a national issue as this study, which focuses on reform of the existing structure of social policies, neared completion. While this study does not address child care, the Institute plans to undertake a separate study of public policy options for this issue.

This study was undertaken as part of the Institute's policy analysis program in conjunction with the Howe Institute Policy Analysis Committee (HIPAC). The Institute believes that the study will make a significant contribution to a better-informed national debate on the social policy issues Canadians face. As with all Institute publications of this kind, the analysis and conclusions are those of the author and do not necessarily represent the views of the Institute or its members.

Edward A. Carmichael
Vice-President
March 1987

# *Acknowledgements*

The origins of this monograph go back to my early years at the University of Western Ontario and to lengthy discussions with colleagues such as Russ Robinson, Jim Melvin, Carl Beigie, Grant Reuber, Ron Wonnacott, and Tom Wilson. In more recent years, I have benefited substantially from the views of, and conversations with, Keith Banting, David Conklin, Al Johnson, Michael Mendelson, Fraser Mustard, Ken Norrie, Doug Purvis, Adil Sayeed, Graham Scott, John Whalley, Ron Wirick, and Bob Young, among others. Various members of the C.D. Howe Institute — Ted Carmichael, Peter Bartha, Wendy Dobson, Barry Norris, and Cordelia Sharpe — were also instrumental. It is a pleasure, once again, to thank Alex Scala for his editing skills.

Research for this monograph began at Western and was completed at Ecole nationale d'administration publique (ENAP) in Montreal. I am grateful for the support both institutions provided. Particular thanks are due to Jayne Dewar for her coordination and word-processing skills and to Western's Centre for the Analysis of National Economic Policy (CANEP).

TJC
ENAP (Montreal)
December 1986

# Introduction

Industrial countries everywhere are wrestling with their social policies. On the one hand, the economic turbulence of the last decade and the ensuing adjustment and restructuring have enhanced the need for a social policy network that is equitable and comprehensive. On the other, there is a growing concern that the welfare state is contributing to weakness on the economic front. In Canada and elsewhere, interestingly, the two aspects of this social policy dilemma appear to be converging into a single broadside against the status quo: according to its critics, the present system is both too expensive and counterproductive, in the sense that it neither facilitates economic adjustment nor provides adequate social and economic support for those most in need.

An example of the welfare state under siege, as it were, is the opening paragraph of a recent overview of the British welfare system:

> There are ten main reasons why the tax and benefit system should be changed:
>
> It is incomprehensible.
> It is uncoordinated.
> It is unnecessarily expensive to administer.
> It is a system of pauperisation, not a welfare state.
> It is a chief cause of unemployment.
> It is deteriorating, not improving.
> It is discriminatory, arbitrary and unfair.
> It penalises marriage, and subsidises family break up.
> It destabilises and divides society.
> It undermines the rule of law.
>
> In short it does not work.[1]

This view is reflected in the opening statement of the comprehensive three-volume British green paper, *Reform of Social Security*: "To be blunt, the British Social Security System has lost its way."[2]

Canadians probably would find this litany too harsh as an assessment of their own social policy network. Nevertheless, each item doubtlessly

---

[1] Hermione Parker, *Action on Welfare: Reform of the Personal Income Taxation and Social Security*, Research Report no. 4 (London: Social Affairs Unit, 1985), p. 7.
[2] United Kingdom, Secretary of State for Social Services, *Reform of Social Security*, 3v. (London: Her Majesty's Stationery Office, June 1985).

would find a substantial number of adherents. Moreover, Canadians surely would add yet another reason for concern — namely, the problems
of coordination, duplication, and even rivalry associated with the federal-
provincial interface in the design and delivery of the network of social
programs. Thus, while the Canadian social security system may not have
lost its way to the same extent as has its British counterpart, the evidence
is mounting that what is needed is a major and comprehensive reform
of social policy in Canada. Indeed, Finance Minister Michael Wilson committed the federal government to just such a review in his February 1986
budget.

The purpose of this monograph is, first, to survey in general terms the
historical and analytical underpinnings of Canada's current social policy
network and, second, to review and assess in detail the various social programs with an eye to ensuring that they are adequate to meet the social,
demographic, and economic challenges of the 1990s. It is hoped that the
result will be a meaningful framework for Canada's ongoing review of
social policy and a meaningful contribution to that review. The remainder
of this introduction is devoted to a brief overview of the study.

One would like to be able, at the outset, to put forward a comprehensive definition of social policy. Consider the following: social policy incorporates the range of policies and programs designed to maximize the
opportunities for Canadians to enhance and employ their human capital. Under this definition, however, social policy effectively becomes syn-
onymous with overall economic policy. Although monetary policy, fiscal
policy, and matters such as the question of Canadian-U.S. free trade have
obvious implications for the well-being of Canadians and their ability to
deploy their human capital, the analysis that follows adopts a more
program-oriented definition of social policy. The focus is on four social
policy subsystems:

- the retirement income subsystem;
- the welfare work subsystem;
- the established programs subsystem; and
- the equalization subsystem.

Chapters 1 and 2 focus on the analytical underpinnings of Canadian
social policy. Chapter 1 describes the historical evolution of social policy both in Canada and abroad. This description emphasizes the manner
and degree to which the development of social programs has coincided
with the emerging set of needs on the social, economic, and political
fronts. The evidence from Canada and elsewhere is that social policy is
no longer well integrated into the broader policy framework; hence, the
rationale or mandate for a comprehensive social policy review. Chapter 2

then looks to the future and outlines a triad of challenges — fiscal, economic, and sociodemographic — that any redesign of social policy must address if it is to serve the needs of Canada and Canadians in the 1990s. The fiscal challenge relates to burgeoning government deficits, both federal and provincial, and the need for all policy, including social policy, to aid in the process of restoring fiscal integrity. The challenge on the economic front is to ensure that social programs become more integrated into the ongoing restructuring and adjustment needs of the economy. At the heart of the third challenge is the recognition that social policy must be reoriented to meet the emerging needs of Canadians arising from changing social and demographic patterns. Associated with these challenges is a triad of trade-offs — adjustment versus security, decentralization versus centralization, the private sector versus the public sector. At the margin, it is likely that the underlying forces in the system will tilt the scales in the direction of adjustment, decentralization, and private-sector participation. Thus, the central task of the present study is to consider how we might redesign social policy within this framework and yet ensure that any new design respects the concern for equity and sharing that is a hallmark of Canadian society.

Chapter 3 provides a brief overview of the four subsystems.

Chapters 4, 5, and 6 deal with the retirement income subsystem. The analysis considers the private and public pension system, the federal income support programs for the elderly — Old Age Security (OAS), Guaranteed Income Supplement (GIS) — the many provincial income and expenditure programs, tax expenditure items such as pension and age deductions, and the tax treatment of Registered Retirement Savings Plans. Although the economic challenge clearly has an impact on this subsystem, the main task of the reforms proposed in Chapter 6 is to strike a balance between the conflicting — and formidable — claims of the fiscal challenge and the sociodemographic challenge.

The welfare work subsystem (Chapters 7 through 11) is defined to include the entire tax transfer and job creation network that applies to the nonelderly — unemployment insurance, welfare, family benefits components of the tax system, provincial programs for the working poor, and so forth. Obviously, all three challenges bear on this highly complex and highly interactive subsystem. The thrust of the reform proposals is to redesign the network of programs in a manner that integrates Canada's needs on the social and economic policy fronts.

Chapters 12, 13, and 14 address the "established programs" — that is, health care and postsecondary education, which constitute a distinct social policy subsystem of their own. If knowledge-intensive industries are the way of the future, then it is essential to link postsecondary education policy with industrial policy. On the health care front, the aging of the

Canadian population has created a fiscal challenge so rigorous that if we cannot find a more efficient, and yet equitable, way to deliver health care services, the consequences for the other subsystems will be severe indeed. The reader will note that the analysis ignores primary and secondary education. This is, admittedly, a defect, justified only by the fact that the primary focus of the study is those areas of social policy in which the federal government has a major role to play in either running or financing the programs.

The equalization subsystem is the subject of Chapter 15. Although federal-provincial interaction characterizes all of the previous subsystems, the complexity of the federal-provincial interface and the implications of the division of powers require at least a modicum of analysis in their own right. In particular, the chapter discusses Canada's equalization program, which is in effect the "social program" for the "have-not" provinces and the basis of their ability to finance and deliver their component of the social programs.

A short conclusion completes the study.

Finally, a personal note. I recognize fully that social policy is an ideological minefield. There are no absolutes that are able to serve as generally agreed-on points of departure. One's perspective on social policy, of necessity, will reflect one's view of the appropriate balance between the role of the citizen and that of the state, between equity and efficiency, and between centralization and decentralization. Throughout the analysis, I shall endeavor to reveal my biases with respect to these and other, equally subjective trade-offs.

At the outset, however, I wish to emphasize two overriding concerns that dominate my perspective on social policy and social policy reform. The first is that social policy has to become better integrated with overall economic policy. Indeed, from any broad perspective, social policy is part of a country's overall economic strategy. Moreover, the relationship is a two-way street: initiatives on the economic front must take account of the social policy context.

The second concern, although related to the first, is more subjective. In my view, the real threat to Canada's social policy network will arise if we attempt to confront the economic and social challenges of the 1990s with a system of social policies that was designed to meet the needs and challenges of the 1960s. Reform is essential not only to ensure that Canadians have in place a social safety net adequate to their new and differing set of needs and challenges, but also to ensure that our hard-won gains on the social policy front in the postwar period can be preserved for future generations of Canadians.

# PART I

## *The Framework for Reform*

# 1

# *The Evolution of Social Policy*

Canada's current social policy network is the product of a complex and often tortuous process reflecting the interplay of social, geographic, political, economic, cultural, and even constitutional factors. In one sense, therefore, the end result is a social policy system that is uniquely Canadian. In an equally important sense, however, some of the critical trends in the development of the Canadian system have also characterized the evolution of social policy elsewhere in the western world. The purpose of the present chapter is to position the Canadian developments in this broader context.

A knowledge of how and why we got to where we are is only one component of the framework needed for assessing and evaluating social policy. The other essential component is an understanding of the needs and challenges that social policy must address if it is to serve Canadians in the late 1980s and beyond. Like social policy itself, these needs and challenges are evolving, and they too reflect the interplay of a wide range of factors. Outlining the nature of these social policy challenges is the role of Chapter 2.

As the introduction noted, Canada is not alone in having to come to grips with new challenges on the social policy front. But it will probably be unique in the way in which it chooses to address them — that is, in the way in which Canadians select particular features of the evolution of social policy to confront the new challenges. It is in this sense that the evolution of, and challenges to, social policy combine to provide the framework for reform.

We begin the process of developing these analytical underpinnings by focusing on the evolution of social policy.

## *The Formative Years*

In a recent article, Hugh Heclo attempts to draw together the historic record of the evolution of social policy in the industrial countries.[1] He identifies four stages in the development of the modern welfare state — experimentation, consolidation, expansion, and reformulation. These four stages are chronicled in Table 1, along with the manner in which each

---

[1]Hugh Heclo, ''Toward a New Welfare State,'' in Peter Flora and H.J. Heidenheimer, eds., *The Development of Welfare States in Europe and America* (London: Transaction Books, 1984), pp. 383–406.

## Table 1
### Stages of the Welfare State

| | Experimentation (1870s–1920s) | Consolidation (1930s–1940s) | Expansion (1950s–1960s) | Reformulation (1970s–?) |
|---|---|---|---|---|
| **Economics** | | | | |
| Events | international diffusion of business cycle; dislocations of industrialization | depression, wartime planning, destruction, reconstruction in austerity setting | unexpected, sustained economic growth | unexpected combinations of recession and inflation |
| Reactions | relief of distress via *ad hoc* exceptions to 'laws' of political economy | integration of social expenditures with doctrines of demand management | intensified commitment to full employment; growthmanship as solvent of economic trade-offs | *ad hoc* attempts to subordinate social policy to a new sense of scarcity |
| **Politics** | | | | |
| Events | workers movements, suffrage extensions, growth of mass parties | discrediting opponents of national government activism | political bidding and group competition for painless policy growth | political disaffection: electoral volatility; distrust in traditional appeals |
| Reactions | policy innovations seeking to accommodate Liberal, Conservative, and Socialist principles | all-party governments in war; emerging consensus on postwar reconstruction | declining necessity for political commitment and building; 'end of ideology' ideology | competition to reduce expectations and avoid unpopularity; neo-liberal attacks on tax, spending, and bureaucracy issues |
| **Social policy** | | | | |
| Form | innovation and volatility in programing 'constitutional' argument on boundary problems | unification of previous experiments | filling gaps and extending inherited approaches | reopening 'constitutional' issues; inadvertent extension in boundaries of social policy |
| Contents | dispensations for the deserving poor and working class; social insurance invented | remedies for risks shared by all citizens | compensations to preserve rising living standards; group struggle for relative shares of increases | marginal slowdowns in spending and programing; low-cost substitute means to seek same social goals |
| Value choices | attempts to reconcile liberty, equality, and security | demonstrations that the 3 values are mutually reinforcing | denial that important value choices are at stake | new recognition of 'tragic' choices; search for positive-sum relationships |

Source: Hugh Heclo, "Toward a New Welfare State," in Peter Flora and H.J. Heidenheimer, eds., *The Development of Welfare States in Europe and America* (London: Transaction Books, 1984), Table 11.1.

was or is influenced by the prevailing paradigms in economic, political, and social philosophy. Although the table is essentially self-contained, some elaboration of the various stages is warranted.

Two important forces facilitated the transition from the stigmatizing nature of most forms of social policy in the "experimentation" stage. The first was related to the social and political aftermath of the Great Depression and the Second World War. The mass economic dislocation of the Great Depression dispelled forever the notion that the need for economic security was confined to a small minority of citizens whose requirements could be met by a highly selective set of relief programs and, indeed, by the "goodwill of relief offices."[2] These societal concerns for guaranteeing more economic security were enhanced by the expected postwar depression and by the homecoming of those who had served in the armed forces — a group so obviously deserving of economic security in return for their valiant efforts.

Combined with these concerns on the social and political fronts was the powerful influence of Keynesian economics on the macroeconomic front. One of the central messages of Keynesian economics was that the economy would not, except by accident, equilibrate at full employment. Hence, it was critically important for governments to undertake pump-priming policies in order to achieve full employment. More to the point, monies spent on social programs would not only aid the recipients but also, via the Keynesian multiplier process, provide greater employment and economic security for all. As Table 1 indicates, for the first time in the evolution of social policy, it became possible to reconcile the broad societal goals of liberty, equality, and security. "Social policy was not only good economics, but the economic and social spheres of public policy were integrally related to each other."[3]

Working in tandem, these events launched the modern welfare state. In the process, the relationship between the citizen and the state underwent a fundamental transformation. In response to the loosening of traditional ties — the family, the church, social and friendship networks, customs and traditions — the state was called on to supplant the traditional sources of protection and economic security.[4] Not only was charity institutionalized but, as Scott Gordon notes, "it was transferred from the realm of benevolence into that of justice," and in the process "the state conferred upon its citizens the right to receive aid from society with

---

[2]Keith Banting, "Universality and the Development of the Welfare State," in Alan Green and Nancy Olewiler, eds., *Report of the Forum on Universality and Social Policies in the 1990s* (Kingston, Ont.: Queen's University, John Deutsch Institute for the Study of Economic Policy, 1985), p. 9.

[3]Heclo, "Toward a New Welfare State," p. 391.

[4]Thomas J. Courchene, "Towards a Protected Society: The Politicization of Economic Life," *Canadian Journal of Economics* 13 (November 1980): 561.

a minimum of reference to the sentiments of compassion and benevolence which activated the older forms of charity."[5] Gordon links these developments to Sir William Beveridge's famous 1942 report on the U.K. social security system (which inspired similar blueprints on this side of the Atlantic). Referring to this report as the "Beveridge transform," Gordon asserts that "it may turn out to be the most significant change in the socio-economic relationship of Western society since labour became a commodity which was bought and sold in the marketplace."[6]

In discussing the evolution of Canadian social policy, Keith Banting[7] argues that this period of consolidation of the welfare state (and, actually, the expansionary phase as well) was characterized by two major processes. The more important was a "flight from selectivity," by which Banting means the adoption of universal programs in the form of either social insurance or demogrants. Banting views the move toward universality as the dominant theme in the development of the Canadian welfare state.

The second process, clearly less important in Banting's view, is what he calls the "modernization of selectivity," typified by the shift from subjective and often stigmatizing *means-tested programs* of the era of experimentation to objective *income-tested programs* of the recent era such as the GIS for the elderly and the refundable child tax credit.

Banting makes a further telling observation about the development of Canadian social policy. The motivating force behind the policy evolution was a "drive for mass security, for predictability, for social rights"[8] rather than for redistribution, which is why Banting argues that the "flight from selectivity" (that is, universality) rather than the "modernization of selectivity" is the dominant feature of the Canadian welfare state:

> Much confusion surrounds discussion of the welfare state and redistribution, especially redistribution between rich and poor. There is a wide-spread assumption in current debate that the expansion of social policy over the last 40 years was intended to carry out a redistributive purpose. In fact, the creation of the welfare state represented a shift away from redistribution as the primary goal of social policy.
>
> Whatever else one might say about the social programs of the interwar period, such as local relief and the 1927 Old Age Pension Act, they were clearly redistributive programs. They were selective pro-

---

[5]H. Scott Gordon, *The Demand and Supply of Government: What We Want and What We Get*, Economic Council of Canada Discussion Paper no. 79 (Ottawa: Economic Council of Canada, 1977), pp. 43–44.

[6]Ibid., p. 44.

[7]Banting, "Universality and the Development of the Welfare State."

[8]Ibid., p. 9.

grams, with means-tested benefits which were financed from general revenues.

In a sense then, the modern welfare state represented a move away from redistribution, at least in the vertical sense. Redistribution was to be from the employed to the unemployed, the healthy to the sick, the non-aged to the aged, and so on. Many of the founders of the welfare state probably thought that as a secondary consequence there would be an important narrowing of the general pattern of income inequality, but that was not their primary aim.[9]

This observation is crucial because, as we shall show later, one of the criticisms of the existing network of social policies is that it does little to tackle income inequality. Banting would probably agree, but he would also argue that it was not designed with redistribution uppermost in mind.

### *The Era of Expansion*

In the era of austerity, the task of consolidating the welfare state required strong and coordinated public policy backing, a condition that was lacking until the Depression and the Second World War mobilized the political and social forces, and Keynesian views on economic stabilization mobilized the economic forces. However, the unanticipated affluence of the 1950s and 1960s changed all of this. Sustained and unparalleled economic growth, by bringing automatic increases in tax revenues or fiscal dividends, rendered social policy expansion almost costless in political terms. Although the network of social programs underwent a veritible explosion, the declining political and economic price of social policy meant that politicians no longer had to strive to build on and maintain the earlier consensus underlying the consolidation of the welfare state:

> After a generation or more of expansion, the democratic welfare states had produced a policy system that was admirably attuned to — and presumed — continuous economic growth. Politically it was a low cost system whose operation generated minimum conflict and maximum, if somewhat passive, support. Economically it was in rough harmony with conventional thinking about fiscal management. Socially it avoided raising difficult questions about social values. *Commitments on the welfare state rose as commitment to it fell* [italics added].[10]

---

[9]Ibid., pp. 10–11.
[10]Heclo, "Toward A New Welfare State," p. 399. The ideas and even some of the phrases used earlier in this paragraph are also from the same source, pp. 397–399.

Canada more than held its own during this expansionary phase in the evolution of social policy. In the 1960s alone, social policy initiatives included the Canada and Quebec Pension Plans (CPP/QPP), the GIS, the Canada Assistance Plan (CAP), the first comprehensive equalization program, the current medicare and hospital insurance programs, and the Department of Regional Economic Expansion (DREE), while the first year of the 1970s saw the comprehensive reformulation and expansion of the unemployment insurance (UI) program. Yet despite this explosion of the social policy network, the cumulative fiscal balance at the federal level during the 1965–74 period was a surplus of some \$2.75 billion!

Several important consequences arose from all of this. First, as Heclo notes in his general survey,

> more and more social policy was assumed to be aimed exclusively at solving social problems: any investment in confronting, debating and resolving political problems (Who is losing and gaining? What are the implications for personal liberty? What rights and duties are owed by whom? Is it worth it?) could be minimized.[11]

Rapid economic growth also meant that social policy could be, and in large measure was, designed without reference to key economic issues such as efficiency, work incentives, and regional adjustment. Given the country's economic surplus, Canada could even afford the luxury of implementing programs — such as the regional benefits component of unemployment insurance, which, as Chapter 7 points out, discourages interregional labor market adjustment — whose very design and intent was to slow down economic adjustment.

Second, with the engines of economic growth humming along smoothly, the nature of the demands on government in the name of "social policy" altered rather dramatically. The original concerns about economic security became appeals to compensate those who lagged behind in the relative income race. Moreover, with the refinement of the principles of economic welfare and social justice, the demands on the state transcended the domain of human needs and entered the realm of human wants. Indeed, they broadened into a very encompassing set of claims — social, political environment, cultural. As Daniel Bell has remarked, "the revolution of rising expectations, which has been one of the chief features of western society in the past 25 years, is being transformed into a *revolution of rising entitlements* in the next 25 [italics added]."[12] Thus, there was a tendency for social policy to move even further from the concep-

---

[11]Ibid., p. 397.
[12]Daniel Bell, "The Public Household or 'Fiscal Sociology' and the Liberal Society," *The Public Interest* 37 (1974): 39.

tion of a safety net designed to facilitate adjustment to a changing economic reality and toward the conception that its role was to provide citizens with something approaching property rights to the status quo.

## *The Reformulation Stage*

The unanticipated economic and fiscal surpluses that characterized the era of expansion were followed by the equally unanticipated economic turmoil and slow growth of what Heclo refers to as the "reformulation" stage of social policy evolution. For present purposes, it is convenient to associate the beginning of this reformulation stage with the world energy price increases that occurred in 1973 and 1974. Since then, the turnaround in fiscal prospects has been dramatic: the cumulative federal fiscal surplus of $2.75 billion during the 1965–74 period became a cumulative *deficit* of some $125 billion during the 1975–84 period (and to one of over $200 billion if that period is extended to 1986). Corresponding to this change in economic and fiscal fortunes was a similar change in the fortunes of social policy. Just as the expansion era allowed social policy to take on a life of its own, the reformulation stage has meant that social policy has fallen on hard times.

The economic pessimism of the past decade has substantially revived the traditional view that there are inherent contradictions among the basic values of the democratic welfare state:

> It [the welfare state] was expensive, so expensive that costs of social policy were themselves posing a threat to individuals' economic security. It was ineffective, generally in providing high standards of service and particularly in making inroads into the gross inequalities of market-oriented societies. And it was dangerous, threatening to pursue welfare at the expense of individual liberty.[13]

The litany of arguments against the U.K. welfare system cited in the introduction reflects the same range of concerns. Moreover, a growing number of Canadians view the social policy network, with its anti-adjustment bias, its poverty traps, and its perverse incentives, as a drain on the wellspring of economic growth. Although I shall not take a position at this juncture on whether or not such concerns are well-founded, the fact that during the expansionary period social policy came increasingly to be viewed as a "residual luxury supported by the nation's economic surplus"[14] surely made it far easier prey than it would have been had it developed as part of an integrated economic and social framework.

---

[13]Heclo, "Toward a New Welfare State," p. 400.
[14]Ibid., p. 403.

Thus, economic stagnation brought about a rethinking of the role of social policy. In effect, concerns over income inequality and poverty rose to the fore — the focus shifted from horizontal equity to vertical equity. As Banting notes, this increased emphasis on vertical redistribution led to a chorus of criticism from both ends of the political spectrum:

> It became commonplace for the political left to argue that the welfare state had failed because the distribution of income had remained so frustratingly stable over the post-war period. Similarly, it became commonplace on the political right to argue that universal programs are wasteful because they are not targeted on those most in need.[15]

This perception, combined with a commitment to the entitlements revolution, led the political left to assert that the welfare system must do more, whereas neoconservatives now assert that it must do less. Banting undoubtedly would claim that, judged by its original objective — a flight from selectivity with an ancillary emphasis on the modernization of selectivity — the welfare system has not failed. But what is afoot now is a general questioning of this objective.

## *Recapitulation*

My own interpretation of the evolution of Canadian policy initiatives on the socio-economic front, perhaps not surprisingly, is broadly in line with the foregoing analysis.[16] The 1960s truly were the good old days. During that decade, the unemployment rate hovered around 4 percent, and productivity increased by 50 percent. The world economy was not only tranquil but expanding rapidly. Canada was nestled comfortably at or near the top of the international ranking of GNP per capita. Given this environment, it is hardly surprising that Canada used its cushion of growth to build a comprehensive and generous network of transfers to persons, businesses, and governments.

It is important to emphasize that, in the circumstances, these policies were quite appropriate. Moreover, many of them were very popular, not only among the target population but among Canadians generally. To put the matter differently, if the underlying economic buoyancy and prosperity of the 1960s still prevailed today, Canadians would not now be engaged in a social policy review.

---

[15]Banting, "Universality and the Development of the Welfare State," p. 11.

[16]This section is based on Thomas J. Courchene, "The Fiscal Arrangements: Focus on 1987," in Thomas J. Courchene, David W. Conklin, and Gail C.A. Cook, eds., *Ottawa and the Provinces: The Distribution of Money and Power*, vol. 1 (Toronto: Ontario Economic Council), pp. 3–21.

But the underlying economics did change. The 1980s are very different from the 1960s. Productivity has been flat for the better part of the past decade, and unemployment has been unacceptably high. Fiscal deficits are nothing short of staggering. In addition, the world economy is anything but tranquil. Economies everywhere are restructuring, and the new world trading environment is becoming more, not less, competitive. The rewards are going to those countries that are able to allocate and reallocate resources quickly and efficiently in response to changing world demands. Indeed, because of Canada's small domestic market, the growing threat of protectionism throughout the world is placing even greater economic adjustment pressures on Canada than on most of its trading partners.

These dramatically altered prospects on the economic front necessarily have substantial implications for the role and design of social policy. Specifically, social policy has to facilitate and assist the occupational, industrial, and often geographic relocation that the new economics requires of the current generation of Canadians. We no longer have the luxury of designing social policy independently of the underlying economic environment. In particular, we can no longer afford those aspects of the social policy network that serve to impede adjustment or to entrench the status quo. On the other hand, the changing demands on the economic front also create new needs that social policy must address.

Where does all of this leave the "economic security" underpinning of the existing social policy network? A large part of the answer to this important question is that there can be little economic security for Canadians in an economy that is slow to adjust. Hence, social policy must become fully integrated with economic policy. In the 1960s, rapid economic growth allowed Canada to mount a comprehensive social policy network; the challenge of the 1980s is to rationalize this network in order to help restart the sputtering engines of economic growth. The other part of the answer is that rationalizing some key aspects of social programs — in order, for example, to remove poverty traps and to encourage work, initiative, and adjustment — is compatible in principle with retaining the basic income support aspects of the social network. Moreover, as a bonus, these changes can be implemented in a manner that, in my view, accords with what the typical Canadian deems to be equitable.

Thus far, the discussion has focused on the ways in which the evolution of Canadian social policy has fallen short of the mark, particularly in its failure to integrate economic and social needs and priorities. There have also been several encouraging developments over the years, however, notably the development of new types of social policy instruments and delivery mechanisms. The GIS, introduced in the mid-1960s, has proved to be a very successful mechanism for targeting benefits to those elderly

Canadians most in need. Moreover, despite the apparent failure of the attempt in the 1970s at social policy reform, the process did give rise to the refundable child tax credit, an instrument that is, in effect, consistent with negative income taxation. The accumulated experience of social policy architects and beneficiaries alike in dealing with these instruments is precisely the sort of analytical and empirical backdrop necessary to devise approaches to social policy capable of accommodating both equity and efficiency concerns. Thus, even if one can substantiate the claim that social policy evolution has largely ignored some of the priorities on the broader economic front, that evolution has also generated new and valuable instruments and delivery mechanisms, which, with appropriate reorientation, should be eminently capable of addressing the challenges of the 1990s.

# 2

# *Objectives, Challenges, and Trade-Offs*

The first section of this chapter deals very briefly with the underlying goals of social policy. The remainder of the chapter outlines in some detail three major challenges that will impinge on the redesign of social policy and the three major trade-offs that all policy, including social policy, must address.

## *Underlying Principles and Objectives*

The report of the Royal Commission on the Economic Union and Development Prospects for Canada (the Macdonald Commission), published in 1985, suggested that although Canadians place a high value on the efficient use of scarce resources, they also bear a broader set of abstract principles in mind when they consider social policies: equity, security, opportunity, responsibility, and sharing.[1] These principles are in general accord with those identified more than a decade ago by then Minister of National Health and Welfare, Marc Lalonde: independence (that is, self-reliance), interdependence (that is, sharing), and fairness.[2]

The obvious next step is to translate these principles into broad objectives for the social policy network. The Lalonde paper, for example, enumerated the following requirements of a "model" social security system for Canada:

1. It ought to be based upon commonly accepted community values, and yet be capable of adaptation to changes in these values....
2. It ought to reflect, not distort, prevailing social and individual values. Examples: income guarantees or supplementation should not be set at such high levels as to undermine the willingness to work; and there should be incentives to work, not disincentives.
3. It must operate in harmony with, not in opposition to, the motive forces of the economy. Examples: it should not seek to sup-

---

[1]Canada, Royal Commission on the Economic Union and Development Prospects for Canada (Macdonald Commission), *Report*, vol. 2 (Ottawa: Supply and Services Canada, 1985), pp. 537–538.
[2]Marc Lalonde, *Working Paper on Social Security in Canada* (Ottawa: Department of National Health and Welfare, 1973).

port incomes beyond the level justified by the productivity of
the economy, nor indeed to redistribute incomes to an extent
which would impair economic growth....

4. A model social security system must be humane and fair, both
   in its benefits and in its administration, in order to help
   beneficiaries to live in decency and dignity....

5. It must be fair as well to the contributors to social insurance
   funds, and to those who contribute through taxation to income
   support and supplementation.

6. It must combat poverty by seeking to assure to everyone an
   acceptable minimum income....

7. It must be equitable as between persons in different situations:
   as between those who are working and those who cannot; as
   between those who are working and those who are retraining
   or are actively seeking employment....

8. The over-all system should be simple and understandable....

9. It should be capable of effective administration and ready coordination....

10. It should be complemented by a system of personal and institu-
    tional services readily accessible to those who need them.[3]

At this level of generality, there is not much room for controversy: most
Canadians would have few quarrels with these ten objectives. The real
social policy debate focuses not on the principles and objectives themselves but rather on the trade-offs among the objectives. To return to the
Macdonald Commission's list, how much emphasis does one place on
"responsibility", and how much on "equity"? In Lalonde's "model" social security system, where does one strike a balance between item 6
(guaranteeing an acceptable minimum income) and item 3 (impairing economic growth)? In other words, the debate is about the manner in which
the objectives are combined or integrated at the system and program levels.

With this point in mind, I shall use the rest of this chapter to discuss
a series of challenges and trade-offs, reflecting the socio-economic environment of the 1980s and beyond, that will, in effect, provide a filter
through which these difficult challenges and trade-offs must be sifted.

Finance Minister Michael Wilson, in calling for a review of social policy in his February 1986 budget speech, enunciated certain principles that
provide just such a filter:

Such [social policy reform] measures must respect several basic principles. They must maintain universal access. They must direct more
resources to those most in need. They must improve the opportuni-

[3]Ibid., pp. 18–19.

ties for individuals to become self-reliant. And they must reduce the after-tax value of benefits going to higher-income Canadians who do not need assistance.[4]

Notwithstanding the homage paid to universal access these remarks would appear to be a call for greater selectivity and targeting of social programs. Moreover, they provide an appropriate lead into a discussion of the three obvious challenges that confront the social policy reform process: the fiscal challenge, the economic-technological challenge, and the socio-demographic challenge.[5]

## A Trilogy of Challenges

### The Fiscal Challenge

The fiscal challenge to social programs is widely recognized, though it is probably uppermost in the minds of those on the political right. The concern is hardly surprising, considering that, at the federal level, the social development envelope accounts for over 40 percent of total federal expenditures and more than one-half of program expenditures. To these direct expenditures, worth roughly $40 billion, one can add another $16 billion or so that is "spent" via tax expenditures or tax credits. With the federal deficit running at about $32 billion and expected to decline only slowly, it is obvious that the fiscal pressure on social programs will be around for some time.[6]

The fiscal constraints on social policy are no less severe at the provincial level. Health care expenditures now account for over 30 percent of most provinces' expenditures and threaten to rise even further under the dual pressures of increasingly expensive diagnostic and treatment technologies and an aging population. As a result, the provinces are scurrying to find increased tax room and ways to reduce expenditures elsewhere. The high-profile reductions in the rates of growth of monies for social programs — in British Columbia, for example — and for postsecondary education — in Ontario, for example — related in large part to the overall fiscal positions of the provinces.

A return to stronger economic growth and a corresponding reduction in the rate of unemployment would no doubt ease the fiscal pressure and

---

[4]Michael H. Wilson, *Securing Economic Renewal: The Budget Speech, delivered in the House of Commons, February 26, 1986* (Ottawa: Department of Finance, 1986), p. 12.

[5]These challenges are based on Business Council on National Issues, *Social Policy Reform and the National Agenda* (Ottawa, 1986), a position paper to which the author contributed.

[6]A brief analysis focusing on international comparisons and the fiscal challenge is presented as an appendix to this chapter.

prolong the status quo on the social policy front. But progress toward dramatic improvement on the economic front is predicted to be long and difficult. Indeed, as I noted above and will set out in more detail below, there is a growing feeling in many quarters that the magnitude of the overall social policy network and the disincentives embodied in it contribute to Canada's inability to perform up to its economic potential.

Without stronger economic growth, the alternative is to increase dramatically the level of taxation. Although some tax increases have occurred already and others are surely in the wings, there are clear limits to this avenue if Canada is to maintain, let alone improve, its competitive position within the global economy. Its marginal income tax rates are already well above those in the United States; in view of the recent federal surcharge and legislation south of the border to lower marginal rates, this discrepancy is generating increasing concern about Canada's ability to attract capital, both physical and human.

It is clear, therefore, that governments at both levels will continue to struggle with their social policy expenditures. The fact that these expenditures will rise as the population ages and that there are new social policy demands on the system suggest that the issue is not whether social programs will be rationalized but, rather, *how* they will be rationalized.

In announcing his intention to engage in social policy reform, for example, the federal finance minister effectively signaled that he is in favor of increasing the degree to which social programs are targeted to those most in need. There are several ways of achieving greater targeting. One is to move away from universal programs and toward income-tested programs. A second is to maintain universality but to tax back more of the benefits that flow to higher-income individuals. A third is to privatize certain aspects of social programs — for example, to place more emphasis on tuition fees in the financing of postsecondary education or to introduce user fees or deductibles for aspects of health delivery.

There is little doubt that as a result of the fiscal challenge, the system will move toward incorporating all of these changes. To be sure, there will be organized resistance to these initiatives, at least initially, since they represent a turning back from the philosophy that dominated the expansionist era in Canadian social policy. The old coalitions undoubtedly will begin to rethink their approach, however, once it becomes clear that the cost of not moving to greater targeting is that some other component of the social development envelope will remain undeveloped or underdeveloped, or that Canadian tax rates cannot be brought more in line with those in the United States. If these coalitions fail to rethink their position, this will not forestall the inevitable: they will simply have (unfortunately, from society's standpoint) a diminished input into the redesign of the social policy fabric.

The Fiscal Challenge and Macro Stimulation: A Technical Detour

It can and should be argued that enhanced aggregate demand is the most effective weapon in the fight against poverty and, hence, in the overall redesign of social policy. The question then becomes: in the current environment, is addressing the fiscal challenge consistent with appropriate demand management? In my view, the answer is Yes. What Canada needs on the macro front is a shift in the overall policy mix, toward tighter fiscal policy and easier monetary policy.

The reasoning is as follows. New investment that incorporates state-of-the-art technology is the key to effecting Canada's economic transformation. Moreover, because Canada's labor force is growing so rapidly relative to that of its trading partners, we need correspondingly more investment in order to maintain the appropriate capital-labor ratio. To get investment up, however, we have to get Canadian interest rates down — both in absolute terms and relative to rates in the United States.

Why not simply pursue greater monetary ease? In principle, easier money should depreciate the spot exchange rate relative to the forward or future exchange rate, thereby generating an expected future exchange-rate appreciation that can then be reflected in lower Canadian interest rates. In other words, an interest rate of 8 percent can be reduced to, say, 6 percent if it is accompanied by an expectation that the Canadian dollar will appreciate by two percentage points relative to the U.S. dollar. The difficulty with this scenario is that, in the current environment, a fall in the spot exchange rate also tends to lead to a corresponding fall in the future exchange rate. Without the existence of an expected appreciation of the dollar, easy money simply results in a lower exchange rate with little change in domestic interest rates. This is the so-called free fall in exchange rates arising from easy money that has concerned the Bank of Canada in recent years.

Quite obviously, the problem is that the world economy does not have sufficient confidence in the future value of the Canadian dollar. The best way to regenerate this confidence is to set our fiscal house in order. Thus, by addressing the fiscal challenge and restoring the confidence of the world economy in the Canadian dollar, easier monetary policy then can be utilized to lower domestic interest rates. In this important sense, achieving progress on the fiscal front is fully consistent with an overall macro strategy designed to enhance both growth and employment.

## *The Economic-Technological Challenge*

The economic-technological challenge — for simplicity's sake, I shall call it the economic challenge — to social policy involves coming to grips with the realities of what may be termed the new world economic order.

To remain competitive internationally (and indeed, to stave off further reductions in Canada's share of world trade), Canadian industry must not only undergo considerable restructuring but also become more flexible and adaptable. The challenge to social policy is twofold: first, to ensure that the incentives within the social policy network will encourage, rather than inhibit, the required adjustment on the economic front; second, to ensure that the social safety net evolves in a manner that reflects the changing needs of citizens as they adapt to the new economic order.

The latter concern first: if the nature of work and the workplace of the future involve greater flexibility or mobility — in occupation, location, or family structure (worksharing) — then it is essential that the underlying social policy networks also become more flexible. For example, if there is an increased tendency for employees to change jobs during their working lives and a tendency for these jobs to be nonunion as well, then pension policy must embody provisions that will ensure that coverage is extended, that vesting occurs earlier, and that pensions become portable across occupations and provinces. As a matter of fact, important recent initiatives in this direction are well under way at both the federal and the provincial levels.

As for the former concern, in the short term there will of necessity be some trade-off between the goals of economic security and economic adjustment. But over the medium and longer term, these goals are complementary, not competing — without economic adjustment there can be little economic security. Hence, to meet the economic challenge, social policy must be reoriented to embody incentives that will encourage both labor and enterprise to embark on those initiatives that will generate a more efficient and competitive economy. Again, an example is instructive. As the later chapters on welfare systems will emphasize, the overall tax rate in the transition from welfare to work can easily exceed 100 percent. Instead of encouraging labor force reentry, the current system is, in effect, generating "poverty traps". Achievement of both efficiency and equity objectives requires that this situation be rectified.

In responding to the economic challenge, however, social policy must remain cognizant of the needs of citizens who are in the process of making the transition. But this should not to be a tall order: surely one of the principal roles of a social policy network is to provide adequate safeguards and fallback positions for those citizens who are responding to Canada's changing economic needs.

## The Sociodemographic Challenge

The sociodemographic challenge is a product of changes in the composition of Canadians who are vulnerable to hardship and in need of protection. New pressures on the family unit have resulted in more and more single-parent families, especially those headed by women. An aging population is putting increasing pressure on Canada's pension and health care systems. Nearly a decade of unacceptably high youth unemployment has meant that many members of the present 25–34 age group have experienced little or no full-time employment. More than in any previous period, significant numbers of Canadians are finding that after 20 years or so of employment, their skills have become obsolete. These and other developments signal a need for reorienting major aspects of Canada's social policy toward the set of needs defined by the current sociodemographic environment. The sociodemographic challenge of the 1990s will not be addressed adequately by a social policy framework designed for the 1960s.

Because of the fiscal challenge, however, it is unlikely that these additional priorities simply can be tacked onto the existing arrangements. Rather, they will have to be incorporated into a comprehensive rationalization of social policy.

## *Recapitulation*

In the expansionary stage of the welfare state, politicians and social reformers had the luxury of designing social programs without concerning themselves much about the manner in which these programs related to the economic system. That luxury exists no longer. In particular, three underlying challenges, reflecting the economic environment of the mid-1980s and beyond, are almost sure to have a substantial influence on the shape of social policy in the future.

The first is the fiscal challenge. The deficit overhang at all levels of government in Canada and substantial income tax cuts in the United States severely constrain the ability of governments to maneuver on any expenditure front, social policy included. Not only are any new initiatives likely to come about only if existing programs are pared back but, even in the absence of new initiatives, there is pressure to find more efficient ways of delivering existing programs. Enhanced targeting is the obvious route to pursue. Moreover, it is likely as well as desirable that, based on ability to pay, financing of some social programs will be transferred from the government to the private sector (individuals and/or firms).

The economic-technological challenge will tilt the social policy system in the direction of facilitating adjustment, both occupationally and regionally. The sociodemographic challenge implies that the priorities of existing programs will have to be altered. The aging of the population means that a greater proportion of social policy expenditures will have to be devoted to the elderly a circumstance that will intensify scrutiny of programs for this group, to ensure that they are effective, efficient, and equitable. Similarly, the growing female labor force participation rate and the increasing number of single-parent families headed by women imply that incentives in the tax transfer and welfare systems must be redesigned to ensure that women's desires to enter or remain in the work force are encouraged rather than frustrated.

## A Trilogy of Trade-Offs

Even if social reformers accept the necessity of redesigning policy in light of the three underlying challenges, the design of any such system must address several important trade-offs. Three of these trade-offs appear particularly important — adjustment versus security, private sector versus public sector, and decentralization versus centralization.

### Adjustment versus Security

The trade-off between adjustment and security — or, as it is often expressed, between efficiency and entitlements — must favor adjustment. The economic challenge clearly points in the direction of ensuring that all socio-economic support systems serve the larger purpose of enhancing adjustment: social policy can no longer be a vehicle for rigidifying the economic system.

In some areas of social policy, this trade-off is not binding at all. As I noted earlier, policies directed toward removing the confiscatory overall tax rate in the transition from welfare to work would increase efficiency and adjustment, maintain economic security, and enhance the potential well-being of those Canadians caught in the welfare trap; moreover, those policies could be designed to increase the degree of equity between the working poor and those on welfare. In other areas, the trade-off is not so benign. The challenge to policymakers then becomes one of finding acceptable ways of modifying entitlements in order to facilitate adjustment. Note that a trade-off in favor of adjustment has application in other areas of public policy as well. It would, for example, affect the inability of younger scholars to obtain university positions because of existing tenure policies and the inability of Canadians to engage in certain activities because of regulatory provisions, such as those that apply in the trucking industry and in various agricultural supply management programs. As Table 1 (in Chapter 1) emphasizes, concerns of this kind illustrate the degree of compatibility among the societal goals of liberty, equality, and security.

To be sure, all Canadians desire a degree of economic security in their own lives and in the lives of their fellow Canadians. It is a natural instinct. Unfortunately, the process is almost surely a negative-sum game because it involves what might be termed the "macro fallacy" or the "entitlement fallacy". This fallacy can be expressed as follows: in an economy where adjustment is an imperative, what may be possible for some groups in the way of entitlements is obviously not possible for all groups. From a political standpoint, the difficulty is that if some groups have been granted sinecures, what tenet or principle can one fall back on to deny similar entitlements to other individuals in society? Given that, as I noted above, there is little economic security in an economy that fails to adjust, it seems clear that the only viable route open to policymakers is to reintroduce some flexibility to these previously protected markets. And the social policy area cannot be excluded. No doubt, the creation of a more flexible social policy will require the use of both ingenious policy instruments and periods of transition. Nonetheless, all three underlying challenges point to the need for a new emphasis on adjustment.

## Decentralization versus Centralization

I suspect that a majority of Canadians would opt for a more centralized social policy system. And in many areas, this choice would make eminent sense. A few years ago, for example, Nova Scotia's welfare costs increased substantially as a result of workers laid off in the energy fields in Western Canada returning to their home province. Should Nova Scotia be responsible for 50 percent of these welfare costs, as it is under the Canada Assistance Plan? Perhaps the federal government should shoulder a larger burden of the income support payments, since what is in progress here is an adjustment to regional and national growth prospects. In a later chapter, indeed, I shall argue for a larger federal role in this area.

In other areas, however, the proper trade-off is more difficult to assess or to determine. For one thing, the division of powers under the Constitution provides some constraints on centralization. Indeed, one of Canada's major contributions to the art of federalism has been its ability to design programs that are national without being central or federal. For example, although the provinces run their own medicare and welfare programs, characteristics such as the elimination of residency requirements effectively link these provincial programs with national ones. The provinces now are implementing new pension legislation that will enhance the national market for labor by increasing the portability, both industrially and geographically, of pensions. To be sure, some of the "national" aspects of these programs are accomplished through the federal government's use of its expenditure power. Nonetheless, Canadians have found ways to create programs that are at the same time national and decentralized.

There are, however, some areas where the underlying challenges are going to impose a greater degree of decentralization. Under the dual pressures of the fiscal and economic challenges, the provinces are already experimenting with alternative delivery mechanisms, administrative procedures, and funding arrangements in areas such as health care, post-secondary education, and welfare. These initiatives will surely intensify in the future. No doubt some Canadians will take a dim view of the provinces' experimenting in various ways with what are regarded as "sacred trusts". But it is important to recognize that what is occurring here is the application of the economic theory of federalism.

One of the principal advantages of a federal system is that it introduces into the government sphere some of the flexibility and competition that characterizes the operations of decentralized markets. The end result of this innovation and experimentation across jurisdictions in the production and financing of public goods and services will surely be that innovations that prove to be superior will be adopted by all jurisdictions. Should one be tempted to downplay the significance of such provincial experimentation, it is instructive to recall that Canada's current health care system owes a great deal to the pioneering efforts of Saskatchewan. That was more than two decades ago, however, and there is now a need to redesign the system to meet the changing nature of the underlying challenges.

It is likely, then, that in the short term the underlying challenges will drive the system toward an increased degree of decentralization.

## *Private Sector versus Public Sector*

Canada's culture, geography, and history all have inclined Canadians to look more benignly on government intervention than do their neighbors to the south. This attitude has some advantages and some costs. For example, in spite of its defects, Canada's health care system is thus far a much better system in most respects than its U.S. counterpart. On the other hand, given a world that appears to place an increasing premium on initiative and adjustment, Canadians may sometimes be too quick to have recourse to government when adversity strikes.

Indeed, "privatization" has recently gained international currency. Every country in the western world and many Canadian provinces are engaged in the process. It is important, however, to view privatization in fairly broad terms. A recent article by David Heald describes four components of privatization:

(1) privatisation of the *financing* of a service which continues to be produced by the public sector: the respective roles of taxes and charges for public services is, of course, an age-old issue but there is now vigorous advocacy of charges playing a much more significant role;

(2) privatisation of the *production* of a service which continues to be financed by the public sector out of taxation: there are many

proposals for contracting out work to the private sector and for educational vouchers which could be redeemed with either public or private sector suppliers;

(3) *liberalisation*, meaning a relaxation of any statutory monopolies or licensing arrangements which prevent private sector firms from entering markets previously exclusively supplied by the public sector;

(4) *denationalisation* and *load-shedding*, meaning respectively the selling off of public enterprises and the transfer of hitherto state functions to the private sector, both thus involving transfers of activity from the public to private sectors.[7]

The fiscal and economic challenges will ensure that the order of the day will be experimentation with all four components. In a series of position papers in mid-1986, the government of Quebec in effect recommended that all four avenues be pursued in redesigning that province's social programs.[8]

In summary, therefore, it seems clear that the pressures on social policy applied by the three underlying challenges will constrain it to favor, at the margin, adjustment and efficiency over security and entitlements, private-sector participation over public-sector participation, and, in the context of "federation economics", decentralization over centralization. In keeping with my commitment in the introduction to make my own biases plain, let me say that I side with efficiency, decentralization, and private-sector involvement. However, the above analysis was not meant to be ideological. My point was, rather, that there is an underlying "determinism" that will push the social policy system inexorably in these directions.

Given this "determinism", the choice of policy instruments becomes all the more important. Indeed, most of the ensuing analysis strives for a more appropriate matching of policy instruments and policy objectives. The proper object of social policy reform is to design a system or set of systems that respects the underlying set of challenges and at the same time works out acceptable compromises among the Macdonald Commission's enunciated principles of equity, security, opportunity, responsibility, and sharing.

---

[7]David Heald, "Privatisation: Analysing Its Appeal and Limitations," *Fiscal Studies* 5 (February 1984): 38–39.

[8]Québec, Comité sur la privatisation, *De la révolution tranquille...à l'an deux mille* (Québec: Editeur officiel, 1986); Québec, Groupe de travail sur la déréglementation, *Réglementer moins et mieux, rapport final* (Québec: Editeur officiel, 1986); Québec, Groupe de travail sur la révision des fonctions et des organisations gouvernementales, *Rapport* (Québec: Editeur officiel, 1986). Henceforth, these reports will be referred to as the Fortier, Scowen, and Gobeil reports, respectively, after the Quebec MNAs who chaired the committees.

To this point, I have used the term "social policy" to encompass the wide variety of income support, income replacement, human resource, and intergovernmental programs that come under the social development envelope. The next chapter provides a classification of social policy in terms of a series of subsystems that are amenable to analysis.

Before I embark on this task, however, it is appropriate in the context of the present chapter to consider one of the "sacred trusts" of the Canadian welfare system — universality.

## A Perspective on Universality

As I noted in the previous chapter, many Canadians would argue that universality is the cornerstone of the present welfare system. The arguments on both sides are well known. Universalists argue, among other things, that the present system was built on the principle of universality: remove universality, and support for the system will dwindle. This argument can be made in another way: if Canada were to remove universality, and to provide benefits only to the poor, the result would be "poor programs". The opponents of universality offer two arguments: first, that selective programs are more efficient and less costly than universal programs and, second, that support for social programs will erode to a much greater degree if we fail to move the system away from universality than it will if the programs become more selective and targeted.

My own view is that the universality-selectivity debate is essentially sterile, largely because it focuses on the wrong issues.

First of all, the debate is frequently a red herring. The only meaningful definition of a universal program is that it is one where, *in the first instance*, the benefits are paid to all (that is, where the benefits are categorical). With appropriate tax-back — or "claw-back" — schemes, however, these universal programs are, in the final analysis, effectively converted into selective (income-tested) programs. Hence, given full freedom to impose a tax-back scheme, then in terms of the ultimate impact on recipients, universal and selective programs become indistinguishable!

The second point is more important. What matters to individuals or families that have to rely on the social policy network is how the *system* of programs affects their well-being or behavior. The fact that *one* program is universal need not make the system or subsystem more effective or equitable. Indeed, it is easy to imagine cases in which the fact that one program is selective completely offsets the fact that another program in the system is universal.

Consider the set of programs for the elderly. This subsystem is not necessarily better because OAS is a universal program. Whether the subsystem is equitable and adequate will depend as well on the GIS, CPP/QPP, the age and pension-related tax exemptions, and the manner in which the provinces integrate their programs — for example, income supplementation and housing — with the federal ones.

Nonetheless, some programs are almost certain to remain universal. But this circumstance has more to do with the fact that it is administratively efficient to deliver benefits universally than with any inherent virtue in universality. Over time, as the technology for delivering benefits improves — for example, as it becomes feasible to deliver income-tested programs more frequently than once a year — we may see a move toward more selectivity. Until this time, however, it is likely that several programs will remain universal.

I shall make little reference in what follows to whether individual programs are universal or income tested. Rather, the emphasis will be on the characteristics of the systems and subsystems of the social policy network.

## Appendix:
## The Fiscal Challenge and International Comparisons

Some might argue that the fiscal challenge is really a red herring. After all, Canada devotes a smaller proportion of its GNP to social programs than do most European countries. Surely, the argument would go, there is room for expansion of social programs in Canada or, at the very least, no mandate for rationalization. Setting aside the fact that the comparisons are conveniently made with European countries, rather than with Canada's principal trading partners, the United States and Japan (with whose spending Canada's compares favorably), I have substantial problems with international comparisons of this kind. The demographics of the European countries are very different from Canada's. As the Macdonald Commission pointed out, the ratio of pensioners to workers in Canada stood at 21.1 percent in 1980, as compared with an average of 28.4 percent in the other countries of the Organisation for Economic Co-operation and Development (OECD).[9] As our society ages, we too shall spend an increasing proportion of GNP on social programs, even without any changes in existing legislation. For example, the proportion of health expenditures consumed by the elderly far exceeds their proportion of the population. Hence, international comparisons are of questionable value unless they are "standardized" to take account of such key differences across countries.

The area where Canada appears to be the most "deficient" in these international comparisons is in terms of pensions — Canada spends 4.6 percent of GDP on publicly funded pensions, compared with an average of 8.8 percent for the rest of the OECD.[10] Again, demogra-

---

[9]Macdonald Commission, *Report*, vol. 2, p. 565.
[10]Ibid., p. 555.

phy explains much of this difference. But so does the fact that, unlike those in Europe or even that of the United States, Canada's public pension system (the CPP/QPP) is not "mature". Projections indicate that the combined employer-employee contribution rate of 3.6 percent will have to rise to somewhere in the 10 to 12 percent range in order to achieve a "pay-as-you-go" equilibrium. The public pensions of other countries are generally already on a "pay-as-you-go" basis, since they were established much earlier.

In addition, these comparisons typically do not take into account "tax-assisted" savings vehicles such as Registered Retirement Savings Plans (RRSPs) — that is, pension tax expenditures — which in Canada are running above $5 billion annually and will expand dramatically when the new, more generous RRSP limits come into play. Finally, at the more detailed level, Canada's public pension system for low-income workers — those whose income is equal to or less than half the average industrial wage — embodies replacement ratios of 100 percent, well above the average of the OECD countries.[11] Where Canada tends to lag behind other countries in its public pension provisions is at income levels above the average industrial wage. But it is precisely at this level where RRSPs and the system of private or occupational pensions are important. Hence, even in the pension area, care must be exercised in drawing implications from these international comparisons.

Indeed, one could make the point that it is only those OECD countries with relatively low ratios of social expenditures to GNP — that is, Canada, Japan, and the United States — that have been able to generate employment growth in recent years. Europe did not create one net job during the 1974–84 period. I am sure that many analysts would argue that it is inappropriate to draw this conclusion without taking account of other factors that affect growth and employment. This is probably correct. Yet, drawing this conclusion from international comparisons is every bit as "valid" as using them to assert that Canada has room to expand its expenditures on social policy.

---

[11]Ontario Economic Council, *Pensions Today and Tomorrow*, Ontario Economic Council Position Paper (Toronto, 1983), Table 14.

# 3

## *Defining the Subsystems*

This chapter provides an overview of Canada's social programs and a link between the general and analytical concerns of the previous chapters and the specific and descriptive content of the remainder of the study. In particular, it classifies the myriad programs in the social development envelope in a manner that not only facilitates their evaluation but also lends itself to bringing the analysis of the previous chapters to bear on the operations of these programs. The chapter begins with some data on the amounts of monies devoted to social programs.

### *An Overview of Social Programs*

Table 2 presents an overview of anticipated federal expenditures on social programs in fiscal year 1986–87.[1] Conveniently, the breakdown of the table corresponds fairly closely to the classification of the subsystems that is developed below. The estimated cost of these programs to the federal government for fiscal year 1986–87 is just under $60 billion, of which roughly $43 billion is in the form of direct transfers and $17 billion is in the form of tax transfers. A substantial component of the $17 billion in tax transfers is in the form of tax expenditures — for example, the married exemption under the personal income tax and the tax cost of RRSPs — which generally go unrecorded in most published accounts of the operations of the federal government.

Table 3 provides a different perspective on social programs. The table consolidates the expenditures of all levels of government and classifies them by the type of program, namely, universal programs, selective or income-tested programs, social insurance programs, and in-kind transfer programs (health and education). Because the years are different, comparisons of the dollar values in the two tables are difficult. However, a rough guess is that aggregate expenditure on social policy in Canada in the current fiscal year is in the neighborhood of $100 billion. This figure will suffice for the purposes of this study, which will place greater emphasis on social policy issues than on the precise amounts spent on one program or another.

---

[1] "Fiscal year 1986–87" refers to the federal government's fiscal year, which ends on March 31 — that is, the period from April 1, 1986, to March 31, 1987.

**Table 2**

*Major Federal Social Program Expenditures, fiscal year 1986–87*
*($ millions)*

| Policy area | Expenditures |
|---|---|
| *Human resources development programs* | |
| Skill development | 1,284 |
| Colleges and universities: cash transfers | 2,380 |
| Tax transfers | 2,423 |
| Job creation | 600 |
| Total tax transfers | 2,423 |
| Total direct transfers | 4,264 |
| *Total* | 6,687 |
| *Income security programs* | |
| Unemployment insurance | 11,500 |
| Canada Assistance Plan | 4,059 |
| Family allowances | 2,531 |
| Marital exemption | 1,385 |
| Child tax exemption | 940 |
| Child tax credit | 1,435 |
| Total tax transfers | 3,760 |
| Total direct transfers | 18,090 |
| *Total* | 21,850 |
| *Retirement income security programs* | |
| RRSP/RPP exemptions | 4,900 |
| Old age tax exemption | 500 |
| Pension income tax exemption | 150 |
| Old Age Security Program | 9,510 |
| Guaranteed Income Supplement | 3,566 |
| Spouses allowance | 605 |
| Total tax transfers | 5,550 |
| Total direct transfers | 13,681 |
| *Total* | 19,231 |
| *Health care* | |
| Hospital care and physicians services | 6,805 |
| Transfer of tax points for above | 5,119 |
| Total tax transfers | 5,119 |
| Total direct transfers | 6,805 |
| *Total* | 11,924 |
| Total tax transfers | 16,852 |
| Total direct transfers | 42,840 |
| *Total cost* | 59,692 |

Note: All tax expenditure costs for individuals are estimated based on 1983 tax returns. Costs for these measures in fiscal year 1986–87 are likely to be 10–20 percent higher due to rising exemption levels.

Source: Canada, Treasury Board, *1986–1987 Estimates* (Ottawa, 1986); Canada, Department of Finance, *Account of the Cost of Selective Tax Measures* (Ottawa, August 1985).

**Table 3**
***Expenditure on Major Welfare State Programs
by All Levels of Government, 1982–83***
*($ billions)*

| Program | Expenditure |
|---|---|
| *Programs without income tests* | |
| Old Age Security | 7.0 |
| Family allowances | 2.2 |
| Total | 9.2 |
| *Programs with income tests* | |
| Guaranteed Income Supplement | 2.4 |
| Refundable child tax credit | 1.5 |
| Social assistance and provincial/local | |
|    income support and tax credits | 6.2 |
| Other | 0.4 |
| Total | 10.5 |
| *Social insurance programs* | |
| Canada/Quebec Pension Plans | 4.1 |
| Unemployment insurance | 8.6 |
| Workmen's compensation | 2.0 |
| Veterans' pensions | 1.0 |
| Total | 15.6 |
| *In-kind transfers* | |
| Health insurance | 22.3 |
| Education[a] | 21.4 |
| Total | 43.7 |
| *Total welfare state programs* | *79.0* |

[a]1981–82

Note: Totals may not add due to rounding.

Source: Ake Blomqvist, "Political Economy of the Canadian Welfare State," in David Laidler, ed., *Approaches to Economic Well-Being,* Collected Research Studies of the Royal Commission on the Economic Union and Development Prospects for Canada no. 28 (Toronto: University of Toronto Press, 1985, p. 90).

## *Defining the Subsystems*

In order to facilitate the ensuing analysis, I have grouped the expenditures on social policy in four separate, although related, subsystems:

• the retirement income subsystem;
• the income support, income replacement subsystem, which I shall hereafter call the welfare work subsystem;
• the established programs system, encompassing health and postsecondary education; and
• the equalization subsystem.

The brief comments that follow on these various subsystems are largely definitional, although I have also made some attempt to relate the subsystems to the challenges described in the last chapter.

## The Retirement Income Subsystem

The components of this subsystem include the private and public pension system (occupational pensions and the CPP/QPP), the income support programs for the elderly (OAS, GIS), the many provincial income and expenditure programs, and tax expenditure items, such as pension and elderly deductions and the tax treatment of RRSPs. Although concerns relating to the economic challenge are not absent from this subsystem, they are clearly not uppermost. The reform process for this subsystem will be dominated by the fiscal challenge and by the sociodemographic challenge.

## The Welfare Work Subsystem

Essentially, this subsystem encompasses the entire tax transfer and job creation network that applies to the nonelderly. It incorporates unemployment insurance, the CAP (welfare), the family benefit components of income taxation, provincial programs for the working poor, low-income housing policies, and job creation programs. The system obviously has multiple objectives and, not surprisingly, it is highly interactive. The proposals for reform will, naturally, respect the multiple purposes of this subsystem.

There is room for considerable improvement, however, in the incentives embodied in the multitude of programs and in the design of the interfaces between them. The sorts of issues that will be uppermost are the following: Is there a sufficient incentive for UI or welfare recipients to reenter the work force? Is the trade-off between equity and efficiency appropriate? Are job creation programs appropriately integrated with the income replacement and income support components of the subsystem? Is the federal-provincial interface conducive to generating a well-integrated overall system?

Given the inherent size and complexity of this system, one cannot claim that the reform proposals that follow are either unique or necessarily superior to other models for reform and renewal. What can be claimed is that the overview is motivated by a concern that this critical social policy subsystem be designed or redesigned in a manner that integrates Canada's needs on the social and economic policy fronts.

## The Established Programs Subsystem

The term "established programs" normally applies to those programs whose financing is based on statutory federal-provincial agreements — medicare, hospital funding, and funding for postsecondary education. One might argue that these programs would be best dealt with separately and not as part of an overall social policy review. On the other hand, the complexity and importance of the federal-provincial financial interface in this area is such that these programs cannot be isolated from a review of the interprovincial aspects of the remainder of the social policy network. Moreover, not only are these programs currently under review but they are bound to loom large in the upcoming review of fiscal arrangements. Finally, the very nature of the fiscal challenge implies that if Canadians cannot find a more efficient, and yet equitable, way to deliver health care services, the implications for the remaining subsystems likely will be dramatic.

## The Equalization Subsystem

Federal-provincial interaction characterizes all of the previous subsystems. However, the complex nature of the interface and the implications for the division of powers are such that it is essential that federal-provincial issues be singled out for special treatment. In particular, some attention needs to be devoted to Canada's equalization program, which, in effect, is the "social program" for the have-not provinces and which underlies the ability of the recipient provinces to finance and deliver their component of the social programs.

## Conclusion

The purpose of the subsequent analysis of each of the subsystems, and of the interactions between them, is to strive for an optimal balance among social responsibility, fiscal responsibility, and economic responsibility, and, as a corollary, to find ways of ensuring that scarce resources are focused more effectively and efficiently on those Canadians most in need. The ultimate objective of the analysis is to ensure that the collective impact of Canada's social policies, both federal and provincial, is of a kind that facilitates economic adjustment and encourages Canadians to seek satisfying and fulfilling employment, thereby contributing not only to their own well-being but also to the dynamism and resilience of Canadian society and the Canadian economy.

# PART II

## The Retirement Income Subsystem

# 4

# *The Status Quo*

## *An Overview of the Subsystem*

As I noted in the previous chapter, the components of the retirement income subsystem include private and public pension plans; the federal income support programs (OAS and GIS); the tax expenditure provisions, such as the pension and age deductions and the tax treatment of RRSPs; and the various provincial tax and expenditure programs. In fiscal year 1986–87, the federal government devoted roughly $20 billion to the retirement income subsystem. Details of these expenditures and a classification of the programs coming under the purview of the retirement income subsystem appear in the third panel of Table 2 (see Chapter 3). Missing from this table are the provincial expenditure components. These would include the provincial share of the tax expenditures — for example, essentially one-half of the values for RRSP/RPP (Registered Pension Plan), old age, and pension income exemptions — and the various provincial programs for the elderly, such as income supplementation programs and free drug plans.

Table 4 presents a more complete description of the retirement income subsystem. Although the table is designed to be self-explanatory, some entries merit elaboration.

## *The Private Pension System*

The last decade has seen innumerable comprehensive evaluations of the Canadian pension system. It would accomplish little to rehash the positions adopted by these various studies; suffice it to say that the result is an emerging consensus on private-sector pensions and legislative proposals that incorporate provisions for greater access, enhanced portability, earlier vesting, enhanced disclosure, fairer treatment of surviving spouses, credit splitting in the event of marriage breakdown, greater employee representation on pension management committees, and flexibility to accommodate early retirement. The fact that jurisdiction over pensions is shared by Ottawa and the provinces makes consensus all the more impressive.

The new pension provisions are both more equitable than the old ones and more in line with the economic-technological challenge (in the sense

### Table 4
### *An Overview of the Retirement Income Subsystem*

| | Who contributes? | Who benefits? | How are benefits determined? |
|---|---|---|---|
| **1. Occupational Plans:** | | | |
| A. Defined Benefit | • both employers and employees in contributory plans, only employers in noncontributory plans | • retiring employees who were with the firm long enough to be vested<br>• surviving spouses in plans with survivor benefits | • specified formula (e.g., final-average earnings, career average, flat benefit plans) |
| B. Money Purchase | • both employers and employees | • same as above | • function of past contributions plus accumulated earnings<br>• pensioner can select various types of annuities |
| 2. RRSPs | • individuals contribute to own or spousal plans<br>• contributions are tax deductible up to a limit | • individuals can withdraw funds from plans before or after retirement | • same as money purchase plans |
| 3. Old Age Security (OAS) | • federal government, out of general revenues | • all Canadians aged 65+ | • flat benefits, fixed by federal legislation<br>• indexed quarterly to CPI |
| 4. Guaranteed Income Supplement (GIS) | • federal government, out of general revenues | • low-income residents aged 65+ | • maximum benefits fixed by federal legislation<br>• benefits differentiated between single and married units<br>• income tested (50% tax back)<br>• indexed to CPI |
| 5. GAINS[a] | • Ontario government, out of general revenues | • Ontario residents aged 65+ with low incomes | • maximum benefit fixed by provincial legislation<br>• benefits differentiated by single and married units, latter are indexed<br>• income tested (50% tax back) |
| 6. Elderly Tax Exemptions[b] | • federal and provincial governments, out of general revenues | • Canadians, aged 65+, with income high enough to be taxpayers | • benefit depends on claimant's marginal tax rate; higher marginal rate, larger benefits<br>• exemptions are indexed |
| 7. CPP/QPP | • employers and employees pay special CPP/QPP contributions<br>• current rate is 3.6%, evenly split | • those 65+, or disabled, who have paid sufficient CPP/QPP premiums<br>• surviving spouses of CPP/QPP contributors | • specified benefit formula, determined more by earnings than contributions<br>• indexed quarterly |

[a]Guaranteed Annual Income System. This program operates only in Ontario. Most other provinces have alternative schemes.

[b]This relates to the age exemptions. The $1,000 pension exemption would be characterized similarly, although it is not indexed. The various provincial tax credits for the elderly are excluded from the table, as are such things as free health care, etc.

## Table 4, continued
### *An Overview of the Retirement Income Subsystem*

| Nature of the contractual agreement | Who administers and controls the plan? | Other characteristics |
|---|---|---|
| • explicit contract between employers and employees, often part of overall compensation package | • generally the employer<br>• some public sector plans tend not to be funded in the actuarial sense[c] | • benefits basically are a function of earnings profile, not contributions |
| • same as above | • generally the employer, although often an employee has some say over how his/her funds are invested | • benefits basically determined by contributions and fund performance, not by earnings profile |
| • between RRSP-owner and financial institution holding the fund; otherwise self-administered | • individual or institution, although inflow of new funds is controlled by individual | • same as money purchase plans<br>• maximum contribution rates have not been indexed |
| • no formal contractual relationship<br>• strong implicit or social contract | • no plan or fund | • basically an intergenerational transfer<br>• universal program, not dependent on work experience |
| • same as above | • same as above | • CPP/QPP benefits are viewed as part of income in terms of being subject to the 50% tax back |
| • same as above | • same as above | • 50% tax-back rate<br>• GAINS benefits are "stacked" with GIS so that overall tax-back rate is 100% |
| • none | • same as above | |
| • no formal contractual arrangement although the public perception is one of contributing to retirement income | • joint federal-provincial plan<br>• surplus CPP contributions invested in provincial securities<br>• QPP also invests in private assets | • until fund matures, current contributors receive a substantial subsidy relative to future contributors |

[c]A better distinction between public-sector pension funds is whether they fall under the category of trusteed funds and, therefore, are similar to private-sector funds or whether they are consolidated revenue funds, which are not 'funded'. For Ontario, the former would include the teachers' superannuation funds and OMERS (Ontario Municipal Employees Retirement System). These are essentially funded plans.

Source: Ontario Economic Council, *Pensions Today and Tomorrow,* Ontario Economic Council Position Paper (Toronto, 1983), pp. 28–29.

that they enhance mobility and, hence, efficiency) and the sociodemographic challenge (for example, in that they enhance spousal rights).

## Registered Retirement Savings Plans

Canadians contributed $5.8 billion to RRSPs in 1984 for a tax loss of
some $1.5 to 2.0 billion at the federal level and roughly one-half of this
value at the provincial level. RRSPs are more than just a pension instrument. They can and are used for income averaging and have been used
to transfer income to spouses. For present purposes, however, the assumption will be that they are a tax-assisted device for enhancing retirement
income.

In his May 1985 budget, Finance Minister Michael Wilson announced
the following changes in the provisions governing RRSPs and private pension contributions (although in his 1986 budget he delayed the implementation date by one year):

• For individuals who have no private pension plans, allowable RRSP
contributions will increase to $15,500 in 1990 from the current maximum
of $7,500, or to 18 percent of earnings, whichever is lower.
• For money purchase plans, the maximum combined employee-
employer contributions to the plan or to RRSPs will also rise to $15,500
in 1990 from the current $7,500. Again, the yearly contribution cannot
exceed 18 percent of income.
• Combined employee-employer contributions to defined benefit plans
will also rise to $15,500 in 1990, with a supplemental RRSP contribution
of up to $2,000.
• For all individuals, there will be a carry forward of unused RRSP contributions for up to seven years.

The implications of these changes are quite far-reaching. First, although
it is difficult to assess the impact that the measures will have on aggregate
savings, it is very evident that savings channelled through RRSPs will rise
dramatically — as will the cost in lost personal income tax revenue.

Second, the enhanced pension and RRSP provisions will be taken up
primarily by middle- and upper-income Canadians. This is evident from
Table 5: not only does a smaller proportion of low-income individuals
make use of RRSPs, but the average contribution rises sharply with the
level of income. The reasons for this are obvious — up to the maximum
contribution level, allowable RRSPs are a proportion of income. Moreover,
the after-tax cost of purchasing RRSPs varies inversely with the marginal
tax rate — a $5,000 RRSP costs $2,500 for the 50 percent marginal tax
rate individual and $3,750 for the 25 percent marginal tax rate individual.

**Table 5**
*Contributions to RRSPs by Income Group, 1979*

| Income group | No. of contributors | Percentage of tax filers | Average contribution |
|---|---|---|---|
| under $ 6,000 | 29,114 | 0.6% | $    456 |
| $   6,000 -   7,999 | 41,092 | 3.3 | 742 |
| $   8,000 -   9,999 | 69,412 | 5.8 | 863 |
| $ 10,000 - 11,999 | 98,928 | 8.7 | 951 |
| $ 12,000 - 13,999 | 118,092 | 11.7 | 1,053 |
| $ 14,000 - 15,999 | 127,813 | 14.7 | 1,218 |
| $ 16,000 - 17,999 | 137,555 | 17.0 | 1,354 |
| $ 18,000 - 19,999 | 143,003 | 20.8 | 1,440 |
| $ 20,000 - 24,999 | 322,965 | 26.7 | 1,672 |
| $ 25,000 - 29,999 | 227,624 | 36.0 | 1,986 |
| $ 30,000 - 34,999 | 145,480 | 46.2 | 2,282 |
| $ 35,000 - 39,999 | 83,650 | 52.4 | 2,594 |
| over $ 40,000 | 181,231 | 59.2 | 3,752 |
| *Total* | *1,725,959* | *11.8* | *$ 1,791* |

Source: Ontario Economic Council, *Pensions Today and Tomorrow,* Ontario Economic Council Position Paper (Toronto, 1983), p. 64.

The proposed new RRSP provisions will exacerbate these trends.

Whether or not these provisions can be viewed as being inequitable depends in part on the philosophy underlying the tax system. If Canada were to move from an income concept of taxation to a consumption concept (as recommended by the Macdonald Commission), then all savings would be treated like RRSPs. Although one might choose to view such a system as being inequitable, RRSPs as such would not pose a problem in terms of equity. Even under an income concept of taxation, a move toward a flatter structure of marginal tax rates would minimize the equity concerns raised by the enhanced RRSP provisions.

Under the income tax system now prevailing in Canada, however, it appears that these initiatives will indeed benefit higher-income taxpayers. Moreover, the generosity of the proposals will have substantial

**Table 6**
*Canada Pension Plan Contributions, 1985–2003*[a]
*($ billions)*

| | Expenditures | Revenue From contributions | From interest | Annual surplus or deficit | CPP fund |
|---|---|---|---|---|---|
| 1985 | 4.8 | 4.7 | 2.9 | 2.8 | 31.3 |
| 1986 | 5.5 | 5.2 | 3.3 | 2.9 | 34.2 |
| 1987 | 6.3 | 5.5 | 3.4 | 2.6 | 36.8 |
| 1988 | 7.1 | 5.9 | 3.7 | 2.4 | 39.2 |
| 1989 | 8.0 | 6.3 | 3.8 | 2.1 | 41.3 |
| 1990 | 9.0 | 6.7 | 4.0 | 1.7 | 43.0 |
| 1991 | 10.0 | 7.2 | 4.1 | 1.3 | 44.3 |
| 1992 | 11.0 | 7.7 | 4.1 | 0.8 | 45.1 |
| 1993 | 12.0 | 8.2 | 4.1 | 0.2 | 45.3 |
| 1994 | 13.1 | 8.7 | 4.2 | − 0.3 | 45.0 |
| 1995 | 14.2 | 9.2 | 4.2 | − 0.9 | 44.1 |
| 1996 | 15.4 | 9.7 | 4.0 | − 1.7 | 42.4 |
| 1997 | 16.7 | 10.3 | 3.7 | − 2.6 | 39.8 |
| 1998 | 18.0 | 11.0 | 3.6 | − 3.4 | 36.4 |
| 1999 | 19.4 | 11.7 | 3.4 | − 4.4 | 32.0 |
| 2000 | 20.9 | 12.4 | 2.9 | − 5.6 | 26.4 |
| 2001 | 22.4 | 13.1 | 2.4 | − 6.9 | 19.5 |
| 2002 | 24.1 | 13.9 | 1.7 | − 8.4 | 11.1 |
| 2003 | 25.8 | 14.8 | 0.7 | − 10.3 | 0.8 |

[a]Assuming no change in contribution rates.

Source: Canada, Department of Finance, *The Canada Pension Plan: Keeping It Financially Healthy* (Ottawa, 1985), p. 4.

implications for the distribution of postretirement income as these individuals age. More on this later.

### Canada Pension Plan/Quebec Pension Plan

The CPP/QPP is the compulsory public pension scheme. Several features of the system are worthy of elaboration. First, the CPP/QPP is not fully funded. This should not come as a surprise. The contribution rate was not designed to cover the full cost of benefits in the steady state. The excess of contributions over benefits in the initial years of the program has been borrowed by the provinces in proportion to their contributions at a rate of interest equal to that on long-term federal government debt. Table 6, which focuses on the CPP alone, shows that the CPP has accumulated a substantial ''fund'' because all working Canadians contribute to the plan, whereas some of the current elderly retired before the advent of the plan and a larger number retired with only partial CPP benefits.

**Table 7**
***Provincial Supplements for the Elderly, 1983***

|  | Program | Year of introduction | Annual benefits Single | Married |
| --- | --- | --- | --- | --- |
|  |  |  | (dollars) | |
| Newfoundland | — | — | — | — |
| P.E.I. | — | — | — | — |
| Nova Scotia | Municipal Social Assistance | 1973 | 219.00 | 438.00 |
| New Brunswick | — | — | — | — |
| Quebec | — | — | — | — |
| Ontario | Guaranteed Annual Income System | 1974 | 586.56 | 1,915.44 |
| Manitoba | Manitoba Supplements for Seniors | 1974 | 187.68 | 404.64 |
| Saskatchewan | Saskatchewan Income Plan | 1975 | 300.00 | 540.00 |
| Alberta | Alberta Assured Income Plan for Need | 1973 | 1,140.00 | 2,250.00 |
| British Columbia | Guaranteed Available Income | 1976 | 466.56 | 1,195.92 |

Source: Colleen Hamilton and John Whalley, "Reforming Public Pensions in Canada: Issues and Options," in David W. Conklin, Jalynn H. Bennett, and Thomas J. Courchene, eds., *Pensions Today and Tomorrow: Background Studies* (Toronto: Ontario Economic Council, 1984), pp. 81–82.

The year 1985 was an important one in the evolution of the CPP: for the first time, benefits exceeded contributions. As Table 6 indicates, however, the fund still shows an increase because of its interest earnings. The fund will not begin to decline until 1994, when the combination of interest earnings and contributions falls short of benefits paid out. In the unlikely event that contribution rates and benefit schedules do not change, the fund will fall to zero in the first decade of the next century.

The available estimates are that, with the aging of Canada's population, a contribution rate of roughly three times the current rate of 3.6 percent will be necessary by 2035 if the CPP is to be self-financing. One short-term alternative is to force the provinces to repay their indebtedness to the fund, thereby forestalling for a while any formal increase in contribution rates. Given the provinces' current fiscal positions, however, this alternative merely amounts to a tax increase of another kind. Indeed, this is no longer an issue, since contribution rates have already begun to increase.

The essential point is that the CPP is seriously underfunded. In other words, to finance the public pension system in the steady state, Canadians are going to have to accept a very substantial tax increase in the coming years — and this tax increase will not reduce the federal deficit, since it is related to future obligations that are not reflected in any of the published deficit figures.

## Provincial Supplements

The only provincial program singled out in Table 4 was Ontario's GAINS (Guaranteed Annual Income System). It is, perhaps, the most interesting provincial program, since it resembles the GIS in the sense that the benefits are taxed back at 50 percent. Indeed, it is "stacked" on top of the GIS, which means that the effective tax rate on any outside income is 100 percent. This issue will also be addressed in Chapter 5.

Table 7 presents a more complete picture of the range of income supplements to the elderly as offered by the various provinces. There are, of course, many other programs for the elderly. Most, if not all, provinces provide them with drug programs, free medicare (in provinces with premiums), housing subsidies, and tax credits of various types. Moreover, many private-sector enterprises offer special concessions to the elderly.

This completes the brief survey of selected aspects of the status quo. The next chapter discusses some of the key concerns associated with the retirement income subsystem; it is followed by a chapter that outlines the reform proposals.

# 5

# *Reform Issues*

The list of potential reform issues relevant to support programs for the elderly is virtually endless. Some obviously important public policy concerns, such as unisex tables for money purchase plan benefits, will have to be ignored here in order to permit a reasonably intensive discussion of concerns deemed — somewhat arbitrarily — to be of even more importance. Specifically, the analysis that follows will deal in turn with the tax transfer treatment of the elderly rich, with the elderly poor, and with the availability of tax-assisted retirement savings vehicles for the working poor.

## *Progressivity of the Tax Transfer System*

With a population that is aging, a key concern has to be to ensure that the constellation of policies for the elderly can deliver a socially acceptable level of benefits in the face of what surely will be growing demands on the fiscal system. As younger people decline as a proportion of the overall population, some reallocation to the elderly from programs such as family allowances and education is possible and likely. A larger reallocation will occur, however, in the form of an intergenerational transfer — from tomorrow's workers to tomorrow's retirees. Given that the next generation of workers already will face a three-fold increase in CPP/QPP contributions in order to qualify for the same *real* benefits as the next generation of elderly, it seems imperative that the additional transfers arising from OAS, GIS, health expenditures, and so forth be perceived to be allocated in a manner that is equitable and efficient.

Herein lies one of the critical challenges to the future of social policy. In part, the issue is the fiscal challenge; at a deeper level, however, the problem is that the current tax transfer system for the elderly contravenes even the most basic concept of equity. Indeed, the current system virtually embodies the problems associated with applying to the 1990s a social policy system designed to meet the needs of the 1960s.

As a starting point, let me assert that the disparities in income distribution among the next generation's elderly likely will exceed those of the next generation's working people. Certainly, the expansion of occupational pensions and the take-up rate on RRSPs implies that a substantial segment of the next generation's elderly are likely to be vastly better off

## Table 8

### Taxes and Transfers for Married Couples Aged 64 or Under and 65 or Over in Ontario, 1982

| Outside income ($) | Marginal tax rate (percentage) | | Transfer income ($) | | After-tax income[a] ($) | | Average tax rate[b] (percentage) | | Net value of OAS for 65+ ($) | Net value of special deductions for 65+ ($) | Total net value ($) |
|---|---|---|---|---|---|---|---|---|---|---|---|
| | 64 – | 65 + | 64 – | 65 + | 64 – | 65 + | 64 – | 65 + | | | |
| (1) | (2) | (3) | (4) | (5) | (6) | (7) | (8) | (9) | (10) | (11) | (10)+(11) |
| 0 | – | 100.00 | 6,540[c] | 12,544 | 6,540 | 12,544 | – | – | 5,684 | 0 | 5,684 |
| 5,000 | – | 50.00 | 335 | 8,224 | 5,335 | 13,224 | -6.7 | -164.0 | 5,684 | 0 | 5,684 |
| 10,000 | 26.64 | 26.64 | 0 | 6,324 | 9,823 | 15,990 | 11.0 | -60.0 | 4,311 | 1,451 | 5,761 |
| 20,000 | 29.60 | 29.60 | 0 | 6,324 | 16,809 | 23,225 | 16.0 | -16.0 | 4,041 | 1,735 | 5,776 |
| 30,000 | 37.00 | 37.00 | 0 | 6,324 | 23,413 | 29,852 | 22.0 | 0.5 | 3,786 | 2,013 | 5,799 |
| 50,000 | 44.40 | 44.40 | 0 | 6,324 | 35,119 | 41,580 | 30.0 | 17.0 | 3,404 | 2,415 | 5,819 |
| 100,000 | 50.32 | 50.32 | 0 | 6,324 | 60,561 | 67,039 | 39.0 | 33.0 | 3,101 | 2,737 | 5,838 |

[a]Transfer income includes Ontario Tax Credits and Ontario Tax Grants for Senior Citizens as well as OAS and, where applicable, GIS and GAINS.

[b]Only the basic personal exemptions and the standard deduction are utilized in the pre-65 tax calculations. Post-65 also includes the old age and pension deductions.

[c]$6,540 = social assistance payments made to unemployable married couple in the City of Toronto plus estimate of refundable Ontario Tax Credit.

Source: Ontario Economic Council, Pensions Today and Tomorrow, Ontario Economic Council Position Paper (Toronto, 1983), p. 185.

than are current retirees. Moreover, it is precisely those with access to excellent private pensions who are most likely to have availed themselves of tax-assisted RRSPs, and to have accumulated private pools of savings as well.

Compared with the present, then, not only will there soon be a larger number of elderly but, more importantly, a significantly increased proportion will be able to count themselves among the well-to-do. It is important that the tax transfer system for the elderly reflect these significant socio-economic and demographic changes.

The thrust of Table 8 is to demonstrate that the existing tax transfer system is very generous — probably far too generous — to the elderly rich. The data in the table apply to an elderly couple in Ontario for the 1982 taxation year. Column 1 presents the level of outside income — that is, market income or pension income — received by the head of the family. Note that, for purposes of the table, all of this outside income is assumed to be received by only one of the spouses. Columns 4 and 5 indicate the amounts of transfer income for the couple before and after they reach age 65. Columns 6 and 7 present after-tax income before and after age 65.

The $12,544 in column 5 when there is no other income — that is, row 1 — is the sum of OAS, GIS, and Ontario's GAINS. The fact that the marginal tax rate for those with no outside income is 100 percent (column 3) reflects the stacked nature of GIS and GAINS. As the level of other income increases, the benefits decrease — since GIS and GAINS are income tested — until they reach $6,324 (column 5), which represents the sum of OAS payments — that is, $5,684 — for the year 1982 plus the value of the Ontario tax credits. Columns 6 and 7 present the difference in after-tax income, preretirement and postretirement. *Regardless of income class, this difference remains in the neighborhood of $6,500.*

Why this is so is apparent from columns 10 and 11. The net value of OAS decreases with income class, since OAS payments are taxable (column 10). But the value of the age and pension deductions increases with income class (column 11), keeping the overall benefits roughly equal in after-tax terms. Indeed, as the final column of the table indicates, the aggregate net value actually increases with increasing income.

The essential point can also be made by focusing on "break-even levels", — that is, the level at which income taxes paid exactly offset the benefits received, or at which outside income equals after-tax income. In Table 8, this income level is $30,107. Only for outside income *above* this level would the elderly couple begin to pay any net positive income taxes.

As I noted above, this calculation assumes that the outside income accrues to only one spouse. Were any outside income to be split evenly between the spouses, the break-even level would rise to $37,000. If any of this income is in the form of dividends or capital gains, the break-even level is much higher still, owing to the preferential tax treatment of these sources of income. Moreover, none of these calculations takes into account the myriad other subsidies for the elderly — drug programs, free medical premiums in Ontario, and so forth. Finally, it should be recognized that one reason why elderly couples can obtain high-income levels is that during their working lives the tax system has provided substantial tax incentives for retirement savings.

It is difficult to escape the conclusion that, overall, *the tax transfer treatment of the upper-income elderly is too generous*. This conclusion is of particular concern because the proportion of the elderly that falls into the upper-income categories is certain to increase dramatically. The substantial improvements in private- and public-sector pension plans, combined with the very substantial and rapidly growing amounts in RRSPs, virtually guarantees this outcome.

## The Working Poor and Provision for Retirement

Precisely the opposite type of problem applies at the low end of the income spectrum. As Table 8 indicates, an elderly couple living in Ontario with *no* outside income would have received $12,544 in benefits in 1982. In 1983, this figure would have increased to $12,735, composed of OAS ($6,099); GIS ($4,720), and GAINS ($1,915). Suppose, again for 1983, that one spouse qualified for a maximum CPP pension of $4,141, but had no other outside income. What difference would this pension income make to the couple's annual income? The answer is *less than $200.*[1] This figure arises because the combined tax-back rate of GAINS and GIS is 100 percent. The only reason why there is any gain at all is that the GAINS support level is slightly less than one-half of the CPP benefit. Thus, if the spouse had qualified for only three-quarters of the maximum CPP pension, the CPP pension would have been worth exactly *nothing* in terms of additional income. In provinces that do not have an income-tested supplement for the elderly, the net benefit of a CPP pension is 50 percent of the benefit level, reflecting the operations of GIS.

To a large extent, relatively high tax-back rates are unavoidable, particularly if the objective is to have a generous, yet highly targeted, income support system for the low-income elderly. In terms of *efficiency*, these high marginal tax-back rates for pensioners are not as serious a problem as they are for welfare recipients, since, even with the abolition of mandatory retirement, there is less of a presumption that the retirement

[1]Ontario Economic Council, *Pensions Today and Tomorrow*, Ontario Economic Council Position Paper (Toronto, 1983), p. 53.

income subsystem ought to be reformed with labor market concerns uppermost in mind. But there may be a substantial *equity* problem, particularly if one views the issue from a lifetime perspective.

In short, the CPP as currently structured turns out to be a very regressive program for those elderly who have no other sources of income — their CPP contributions generate very little in the way of additional income in retirement. Moreover — and here some considerations of efficiency enter the picture — the impact of the 3.6 percent CPP payroll tax diminishes the current employment prospects of these low-income workers. When this tax rises to the 11 percent or so necessary for "pay-as-you-go" equilibrium, this impact may well be substantial.[2]

There is a certain irony here. The CPP/QPP is portrayed in many quarters as the most "equitable" pension plan. In terms of coverage and of facilitating mobility, the public pension plan does indeed score high marks. But it does not score high marks in terms of benefiting low-income Canadians, largely because of the manner in which it is integrated into the benefit system for the elderly. The subsidy to today's contributors associated with the underfunding of the program will accrue primarily to middle- and upper-income Canadians and will be financed by tomorrow's rich *and* poor contributors.

The principal problem for today's working poor and unemployed is *current income*, not future income. Yet, the CPP/QPP diminishes current income — in terms of both take home pay and employment opportunities — while doing little to enhance future or retirement income. Here is a case where society's concern over future income may well be serving to diminish the current income prospects of the lowest quintile of the income distribution. One solution to this problem would be to have the CPP become applicable only at, say, age 25 or 30 unless the earnings exceed a certain threshold. Certainly, the level of earnings that currently triggers CPP contributions — $2,580 — is too low. Compounding this problem is the fact that pension payments — whether of the CPP, occupational, or RRSP type — are treated as deductions rather than as credits for tax purposes. Hence, *low-income earners get little or no tax relief at the contribution end, while, as I noted above, the tax rates can be confiscatory at the benefits end.*

With this brief overview of some of the social policy issues underlying the present retirement income arrangements, we now turn to the proposals for reform.

---

[2]See Henri-Paul Rousseau and François Taurand, "Taxes sur la masse salariale et emplois: le cas du Québec," Faculté des sciences sociales cahier 3809 (Québec: Université Laval, 1983).

# 6

# Reform Proposals

## Approaches to Reform

### The Big Bang Approach

There are two general approaches one can take to reform, whether in reference to the retirement income subsystem or to other social policy areas. One approach is to focus on the various subsystems and recommend subsystem-specific changes in response to fiscal, sociodemographic, or economic challenges. This approach may be called incrementalism. The other approach is to aim for universal reform — the "big bang" approach.[1]

In the present context, the typical big bang approach is a call for some version of a universal guaranteed annual income (GAI) or a negative income tax (NIT).[2] Just such a call went up the last time Canada embarked on social security reform and, interestingly enough, a universal scheme was also the centerpiece of the Macdonald Commission's reform proposals. Since many social reformers still argue for the universal approach, it is useful to focus on why the attempts in this direction in the 1970s failed.

The review of social security in the 1970s effectively began with the 1970 White Paper, *Income Security For Canadians*, issued by then Minister of National Health and Welfare John Munro, followed by Marc Lalonde's 1973 *Working Paper on Social Security In Canada*. In terms of the evolution of social policy (see Table 1 in Chapter 1), these proposals can be situated near the end of the expansionist phase of the development of the welfare state. Canada had just come through the social policy explosion of the middle and late 1960s; now the federal government sought, in effect, to "rationalize" the entire system by embarking on

---

[1]See Michael Mendelson, "Rationalization of Income Security in Canada," in Thomas J. Courchene, David W. Conklin, and Gail C.A. Cook, eds., *Ottawa and the Provinces: The Distribution of Money and Power*, vol. 1 (Toronto: Ontario Economic Council, 1985), pp. 229–252.

[2]I shall employ the terms GAI and NIT interchangeably to refer to a scheme that incorporates a minimum income level adjusted for family size with a tax-back rate on any "outside" or "market" income. Obviously, there will be an infinite variety of such schemes, depending on the choice of the guarantee level, the tax-back rate, and, hence, the "break-even" income level where the family unit begins to pay "positive" income taxes.

a comprehensive NIT or GAI. To oversimplify somewhat, the federal strategy was to "buy out" the provinces — or, rather, to make them an offer that they could not refuse. If we view the matter from this perspective, it is clear that the initiative faltered in large part because the federal fiscal position deteriorated quite remarkably during the 1973–78 period. What might have been possible in the 1970–73 era became unrealistic as federal budgetary surpluses turned into substantial deficits. In terms of fiscal reality, Prime Minister Trudeau's austerity program in the aftermath of the 1978 Bonn Summit effectively put an end to the reform process.

There were other problems as well. Although the initiative was federal, the process embodied full federal-provincial interaction and consultation. One of the ultimate stumbling blocks was that a full-blown NIT would have required Ottawa and the provinces alike to tailor any future changes to the income tax system to NIT concerns, since the tax system was to be the backbone of the delivery system. In the final analysis, this requirement proved to be too constraining for many of the provinces.

This time around, the process of reform is operating within very different parameters. First, chronic federal fiscal deficits mean that there is no money to "buy out" the provinces. Indeed, although the provinces are likely to be consulted and encouraged to join in the process, the commitment to reform is basically a federal commitment. What this implies is that grandiose schemes that would incorporate provincial welfare programs probably are not in the cards.

Moreover, it is not even obvious that universal proposals such as a GAI or an NIT are the best approach. The challenges inherent in the retirement income subsystem are quite different from those operating in the welfare work subsystem: concerns over efficiency loom large in the latter case, but are not particularly relevant in the former. Hence, it is unlikely that a single, universal program would be able to incorporate the multiple goals and needs of a social policy network adequate for the 1990s. To the extent that a GAI attempts to do just this — for example, by gearing benefit levels to accommodate those groups that cannot, for whatever reason, enter the labor force — the result is typically either that the overall proposal becomes far too generous for other beneficiaries or, if the cost is to be kept down, that the resulting tax-back rates are so high that they defeat the original rationale (to encourage labor force reentry for example) for a GAI. Indeed, Chapter 10, which focuses on the Macdonald Commission's GAI proposals, will conclude that they are far too expensive.

In short, the time is not quite ripe for a big bang approach. The monitoring and delivery technology necessary for a full-blown NIT is not as yet sufficiently developed. More importantly, the current range of programs, both federal and provincial, in the income support, income replacement arena is such that they cannot be incorporated easily into an NIT scheme that, at the same time, would respect fiscal, economic, and sociodemographic challenges. In other words, an evolutionary, rather than revolutionary, approach to social policy reform is called for.

This said, however, there is little doubt that social policy in Canada and elsewhere will evolve in directions consistent with the eventual implementation of a GAI. Thus, there is considerable value to keeping GAI instruments in mind when redesigning the various subsystems, particularly in light of the obvious coordinating and integrating roles that they serve so well. Indeed, the recent evolution of Canadian social policy points inexorably in this direction: the one very important building-block that did emerge from the review of the 1970s was the refundable tax credit, an NIT instrument *par excellence*.

## Tax Reform

An alternative approach to social policy reform would be to incorporate it in the larger context of the reform of the tax system. Quite independently of recent U.S. developments on the tax front, Canada has been considering seriously the adoption of a value-added tax (VAT) — the so-called business transfer tax (BTT) — as part of a reform of the manufacturers' sales tax and as part of an overall strategy to derive more tax revenue from consumption rather than income sources. Now that the United States has lowered marginal tax rates dramatically and shifted tax revenues away from personal and toward corporate income taxation, the pressure on Canada to revamp its personal income tax (PIT) system will increase.

There is no question that social policy reform is more easily accomplished in the context of a tax system that incorporates base broadening and a lowering of marginal rates. Under such a system, the income distribution concerns relating to disparities in the after-tax cost of RRSPs, for example, could be greatly ameliorated. Moreover, with a VAT and a revised corporate tax system playing a larger revenue-raising role in the system, the PIT would gain an extra degree of freedom in its role as the means for delivering a coordinated income support system.

This possibility presents the policy analyst with an uncomfortable dilemma. The kinds of social policy reforms that are possible and desirable in the context of the existing PIT system may not be the first-best solutions under the assumption that Canada also will embark on tax reform. As a result of this dilemma, the approach in this study to social policy reform will focus on the needs of the subsystem under consideration with the following two provisos:

• other things being equal, the emphasis will be on instruments that are consistent with the adoption of a full-blown GAI sometime in the future;

• again, other things being equal, the emphasis will be on modifications consistent with the adoption of a flatter PIT structure.

With these provisos in place, the rest of this chapter will consider proposals for reforming the retirement income subsystem.

## *The Tax Transfer System*

The fact that two couples, one earning $10,000 and the other $100,000, both have an after-tax income roughly $6,000 more after age 65 than before age 65 is clear evidence that the tax transfer system for the elderly is too generous for those with high incomes.

One argument that has received considerable currency in reform circles is that the OAS has outlived its usefulness and should be replaced by an expanded GIS. As of 1979, such a change would have resulted in savings of over $1 billion, while maintaining the same guaranteed income level for the elderly.[3] An alternative proposal, recommended by the C.D. Howe Institute, is to tax back the OAS payments according to a separate tax schedule.[4]

Both of these proposals merit serious consideration. There is, however, a further alternative, one that respects the role of OAS payments as part of the "sacred trust" of the social security system. The first component of this reform would be a *gradual* elimination of both the old age and pension deductions. As Table 8 (in Chapter 5) indicates, this change would mean that an elderly couple with an income of $100,000 eventually would be assessed an additional $2,737 in taxes (column 11). The initiative would not affect very low-income pensioners; hence, this modification is a very "progressive" one. It is also one that would generate increasing revenues as Canadians with substantial private pensions and RRSPs (which are already tax-assisted) reached retirement age.

The second component of the reform would be the indexation for inflation of the aggregate of GIS and OAS, with the resulting increment being devoted entirely to the GIS component. Under this scheme, OAS would remain fixed in nominal terms, but it would decline gradually in real terms. This measure also would increase the degree to which the elderly benefits are targeted to those most in need.

The third component of the reform package would be the allocation of some of the tax savings to the enhancement of GIS, so that those elderly

---

[3]See, for example, Dr. Peter H. Pearse in a dissenting comment in Economic Council of Canada, *One in Three: Pensions for Canadians to 2030* (Ottawa: Supply and Services Canada, 1979), p. 113.
[4]Edward A. Carmichael, *Tackling the Federal Deficit*, Observation no. 26 (Toronto: C.D. Howe Institute, 1984), p. 39.

in the lowest quintile would be made better off than they are under the status quo.

The final component of the package would be the use of the remainder of the savings to reduce marginal tax rates across the board. This decrease in marginal tax rates, which would be further enhanced by savings elsewhere in the social security system, would be important not only because it would compensate the middle- and upper-income classes for the tax increases inherent in making the benefits more selective, but also because it would help Canada meet the challenge of sharply reduced PIT marginal rates in the United States.

This, then, is a reform package that would address the three major challenges as they relate to the retirement income system. The savings would be substantial, and the system also has much to recommend it on income-distribution or ability-to-pay grounds. In order to make the package marketable politically, some portion of the overall savings could, as noted, be used to top up GIS. Overall, then, this reform would amount to an internal income transfer among the elderly. The lower echelons would be made better off by a gradual reduction in the benefits to those who, by any standard one might apply, are not in need of government income supplementation.

The federal government may well be a bit reluctant to tackle reform of the tax transfer aspects of the retirement income subsystem in the wake of the unsuccessful initiatives in the May 1985 budget. I am confident, however, that such a reform package would receive substantial support, especially if it were implemented gradually. After all, for the system to remain acceptable and viable in light of the aging of Canada's population, it is important that the perception exist that "both the workers who pay taxes and the elderly who receive benefits are treated fairly."[5]

## *The Working Poor and the Retirement Subsystem*

The working poor are not well positioned to take full advantage of the various features of the retirement subsystem. To be sure, the OAS/GIS combination provides them with a reasonably generous fallback position if they reach retirement without other sources of income. However, the incentives for retirement savings are much more valuable to high-income than to low-income individuals.

In order to rectify this situation, the following options appear appropriate:

• The proposed substantial increases in the allowable retirement pension contributions should be implemented as a tax credit (at 30 percent,

---

[5]Ibid., p. 40.

for example), rather than as an income tax deduction. This measure would preserve the status quo in terms of the current $5,500 maximum; it also would ensure that any contributions beyond this level would be deductible only to the extent of 30 percent. This arrangement is clearly appropriate in terms of both ability-to-pay considerations and the fiscal challenge.

• Those whose marginal tax rate is less than 30 percent should have the option of using the 30 percent tax credit for any and all RRSP, CPP/QPP, or registered retirement contributions. This measure would enhance the incentives for the working poor to contribute to their retirement.

• There should be some overall minimum lifetime threshold value for tax-assisted savings up to which all Canadians have the right to contribute. What this implies is that if workers who spent most of their working lives in low-paying jobs finally find their fortunes improved, they should have the opportunity to make contributions up to the threshold level.

Finally, there is a further matter germane to the fortunes of the working poor that is worrisome. Evidence from Quebec suggests that a 1 percentage point increase in the payroll tax would cost that province 5,000 jobs.[6] Were these results to hold for Canada, a 1 percentage point increase in payroll taxes would result in 20,000 fewer jobs. Given that the CPP/QPP contributions will gradually increase from 3.6 percent to somewhere in the 10 to 12 percent range, this evidence is cause for serious concern. At the very least, more research in this area is warranted. Although it is important that workers have improved prospects for their retirement years, it is also critical that this not be at the expense of their current income. This consideration is especially important in the case of younger, low-income workers. If the effects of increased CPP/QPP contributions on employment are indeed very deleterious to this group, then the appropriate policy is to raise, substantially, the income threshold at which the CPP/QPP becomes applicable. As I noted earlier, this measure also would reduce the regressivity associated with the CPP/QPP for low-income workers.

There is one further issue looming on the horizon that could overwhelm the status quo as it relates to the retirement income subsystem: the abolition of mandatory retirement.

## *The Abolition of Mandatory Retirement*

Most existing social policy programs in the retirement income subsystem assume, implicitly or explicitly, that individuals retire at some specific

---

[6]Henri-Paul Rousseau and François Taurand, "Taxes sur la masse salariale et emplois: le cas du Québec," Faculté des sciences sociales cahier 3809 (Québec: Université Laval, 1983).

age, normally 65. If this assumption is overthrown, as it already has been in some provinces, it may complicate severely the operations of the retirement income subsystem. For some programs, such as money purchase pension plans, the concerns are minimal, since the accumulated value of the pension account is known with certainty at each point in time. More serious problems may be associated with defined benefit plans, since the amount of pension "purchased" with each year's contribution traditionally assumes a specific retirement date. But even here solutions probably will not be hard to come by.

The real source of concern would appear to be the overlap between the private and public sectors. If mandatory retirement disappears, will OAS and the pension and old age deductions still come in at age 65? Now that the CPP/QPP can be taken on a reduced scale at age 60, will the age and pension exemption also begin at 60? Can a worker claim a CPP/QPP at age 65 even if he or she remains on the job? What notion of equity is invoked when one worker retires at age 60 with a reduced CPP/QPP but with no OAS or age or pension deductions, while another worker remains on the job after 65 with a full CPP/QPP and OAS and the age and pension deductions?

The social policy architects may very well be able to think their way through this maze. It would appear, however, that proposals along the lines of those elaborated earlier would be even more attractive in a no-mandatory-retirement environment. Indeed, one could go even further and suggest that the ultimate solution would be an income-tested GAI for the elderly. The earlier recommendations for phasing out the age and pension exemptions, for placing greater emphasis on GIS relative to OAS, and for enriching somewhat the overall support level for the low-income elderly would move the system in the direction of providing an environment within which a flexible approach to retirement could be accommodated more easily. The scheme would provide individuals with an incentive to remain in the labor force if they so desired, and it would also provide the various levels of government with flexibility in determining when and how support for the elderly would come into full play. In other words, it would serve to downplay somewhat the concept of a retirement age in terms of the public pension system in a way that mirrors what is happening in the work environment.

As I said above, the long-term solution may well be a full-blown GAI covering the entire age spectrum. What the elimination of mandatory retirement implies is that an NIT approach for the elderly may become appropriate at an earlier date. This remedy effectively would remove any concept of retirement age from the system. It is here, however, that a justification appears for the earlier emphasis on (a) incrementalism and (b) those design changes that eventually can accommodate the establishment of a GAI. It seems clear that the existing constellation of social programs will not be suited to the needs of the next generation of elderly. At the same time, it is not clear whether elimination of mandatory retirement will generate a sea change in the attitudes of the elderly. The proposals formulated for this subsystem have the virtue that they address some of the more pressing concerns without locking in any preconceptions of how the system might, or ought to, evolve.

## Provincial Programs

The reform proposals put forward so far have focused on the tax transfer system. There are, however, many other programs for the elderly that make use of the fiscal expenditure system. Most of them operate at the provincial level. Free drug programs and exemption from medical premiums (in Ontario) are valuable and, indeed, necessary for some sub-groups of the elderly. However, the same principles apply here: the universal nature of these programs implies that, to an increasing degree, the benefits will go to individuals or families that have the ability to pay a portion of the relevant costs. I shall offer several examples in the health care area in the chapters dealing with the established programs. One will suffice for now: exemption from medical premiums could be converted into a taxable benefit, so that those in the middle- and upper-income classes contribute their fair share toward the financing of the health care program.

There is a second aspect of provincial programs for the elderly that requires rethinking: the manner in which the programs interact with federal programs. The interaction of Ontario's GAINS program with the GIS implies that, over a substantial range, the tax rate on any outside income is 100 percent. The problem with confiscatory tax rates is not only that they are perceived to be grossly unfair but also that they tend to generate creative avoidance systems. In addition, as I noted earlier, for elderly families with no other sources of outside income other than the public pension system, the combination of GAINS-GIS effectively reduces to zero the value of lifelong contributions to the CPP. This situation can be rectified easily through instrument redesign or better GAINS-GIS integration. The marvel is that the status quo in this regard has persisted for so long.

In principle, this discussion completes the evaluation and redesign of the retirement income subsystem. The analysis has been limited to the existing range of policies, and the proposals for reform have been framed with due regard for the three underlying challenges and for concerns relating to equity both across generations and in terms of income distribution among the elderly. However, the political winds appear to be blowing in the direction of introducing yet another program for the elderly, namely, an extension of CPP/QPP systems to encompass "homemakers". Recent polls have suggested that a majority of Canadians favor such an

extension. This being the case, it is important that some attention be directed to the proposals for a homemakers' pension.

## A Homemakers' Pension

Much of the debate surrounding the issue of a homemakers' pension
is highly political. Important as the political considerations are, they will
not be discussed here. Instead, the analysis will focus on the manner in
which the provision of a homemakers' pension would affect the retirement income subsystem.

First, a general comment. Incorporating a homemakers' pension as part
of the CPP/QPP would move the public pension system in the direction
of becoming an omnibus social program and away from its present status
as an earnings-related contributory pension plan; in other words, the
CPP/QPP would move away from its social insurance function and toward
a general income support function. A change of this kind almost certainly would undermine the CPP/QPP in much the same way as loading unemployment insurance with all sorts of ancillary social goals has served
to undermine support for UI.

Second, in its initial stages a homemakers' pension, like the current
CPP/QPP system, would be highly subsidized, since, initially, there would
be contributors but no beneficiaries. Because the take-up rate would favor
higher-income families, and because the impact of such a CPP on the
retirement incomes of the elderly poor would be minimal (for the reasons given earlier), the subsidies in such a system would be quite
perverse — to tomorrow's middle- and upper-income retired homemakers from tomorrow's working poor. The nature of the overall fiscal
challenge surely would rule out embarking on a program with these
income distribution characteristics.

Third, if one were to introduce a homemakers' pension, Canada would
be in the peculiar position of having *two* full-blown social security systems for the elderly — the OAS-GIS combination and the CPP/QPP system, both of which then would cover the entire spectrum of the elderly.

If there is a political will to introduce a homemakers' pension, however,
then there is one approach that might meet the criteria underlying the
analysis of the retirement income subsystem. This would be to *merge* the
two systems. Indeed, an argument could be made for such a merger even
under the present system, although the earlier analysis did not opt for
this route. But if a homemakers' pension were tacked on to the CPP/QPP,
the argument would become more persuasive.

The characteristics of the merged retirement income system would be
as follows. With a homemakers' pension in place, the CPP/QPP would
become *the* universal benefit scheme for the elderly. Contributions would
follow current practice except that, beyond a certain income threshold,

workers also would have to contribute to a CPP/QPP for their spouses, unless they were contributing in their own right. At retirement age, *all citizens* would be entitled to a *single* universal payment equal to the *maximum* CPP/QPP benefit level. The OAS would disappear — that is, it would be folded into the CPP/QPP and the latter, as noted, would become the universal component of the subsystem. The GIS would remain in place but, as above, the age and pension provisions gradually would be eliminated. The subsidies in this new system would be in the "right" direction. The poorest level of the work force would not have to contribute as much over their working lives to receive the universal payment as would higher-income workers. In effect, this system would bring Canada back to that period when OAS was financed in part by an annual income tax surcharge.

Under a system of this kind, one might be able to support the introduction of a homemakers' pension. The approach outlined here would not only rationalize the present system but also instill the concept that a portion of the universal component of the retirement system has to be "earned" on the basis of ability to pay. The likelihood is that such a proposal would not be marketable politically, despite some obvious merits. In my view, however, the notion of simply incorporating a homemakers' pension into the present system is also not acceptable, either on income distribution grounds or — given the substantial underfunding of the existing CPP/QPP — in terms of the fiscal challenge.

The discussion now shifts to the welfare work subsystem, far and away the most complex of the subsystems and the one most in need of reform.

# PART III

## The Welfare Work Subsystem

# 7

# *Unemployment Insurance*

## *The Approach to the Subsystem*

The welfare work subsystem encompasses the range of social assistance and social insurance programs relating to the nonelderly. Each of the three major components of the subsystem — unemployment insurance, welfare or the Canada Assistance Plan, and the tax transfer system of family benefits — is the subject of a separate chapter. As it did in the case of the retirement income subsystem, the analysis focuses in turn on the status quo, on the pressures for reform, and on the principles guiding the redesign or reform process. The final two chapters of Part III draw together the recommendations for each of the major components and integrate them into an overall package. Actually, the first of these overview chapters is essentially an elaboration and evaluation of the comprehensive reform packages for the welfare work subsystem proposed by the Macdonald and Forget Commissions. The final chapter presents my preferred package of reforms and an analysis of the subsystem impacts, such as the financial and economic interactions among the various components and the resulting fiscal interaction between the two levels of government.

The present chapter discusses unemployment insurance, the first of the three major components of the welfare work system.

## *The Status Quo[1]*

### *The Range of Programs under UI*

In 1984, benefits under the unemployment insurance program amounted to some $11.2 billion. Of this total, employee and employer contributions financed just under $8 billion; the remainder came from the federal government's consolidated revenue fund. In addition to the "core"

---

[1]The *Report* of the Commission of Inquiry on Unemployment Insurance (the Forget Commission) was made public after the present monograph was submitted for publication. The Forget Commission and its recommendations, however, are too significant to be ignored. Hence, the following compromise was struck. The original analysis of UI would remain essentially intact, drawing only sporadically from the findings of the Forget Commission. A more detailed analysis and evaluation of these findings appears in Chapter 10, which was devoted originally to an evaluation of the Macdonald Commission's recommendations.

of UI, the system over the years has come to be the delivery mechanism for several associated programs. Most prominent, of course, are the provisions for regionally extended benefits and the special benefits for self-employed fishermen. The cost of these two programs for 1984 was nearly $3 billion. The maternity and sickness benefits component of UI accounted for roughly $20 million and $40 million respectively. Finally, the UI program also incorporates the so-called developmental uses of UI benefits: sections 37, 38, and 39 of the *Unemployment Insurance Act* allow benefits to be deployed to encourage or facilitate work sharing, job creation, and skill training activities. As a result of all of these associated features, UI has moved away from being a pure social insurance program and toward becoming an all-purpose socio-economic program. In turn, this process has led, quite appropriately, to a general questioning of whether the UI program is the most appropriate vehicle for delivering some or most of these associated programs. Moreover, as I shall demonstrate below, the impact of loading ancillary programs onto UI has resulted in a pattern of benefits that, viewed from virtually any perspective, is inequitable. To put the matter differently, the increasingly multipurpose and multifunction nature of UI is eroding popular support for the entire program.

## *The Mechanics of UI*

### Eligibility Requirements

For UI purposes, Canada is divided into 48 "economic regions". The number of weeks of insurable employment to qualify for UI benefits varies with the rate of unemployment in these economic regions. Where the unemployment rate is above 9 percent, ten weeks of insurable employment are required. As the unemployment rate falls, more weeks of insured employment are necessary to qualify for benefits: the maximum number of required weeks is 14, in regions where the unemployment rate is 4 percent or lower.

### Benefit Duration

The duration of benefits is determined as follows. In phase I of the program, which covers the first 25 weeks of employment, each week of employment generates one week of eligibility for benefits. In phase II, which covers employment beyond 25 weeks, each two weeks of employment generates one week of eligibility, up to a maximum of 13 weeks of eligibility. Regional extended benefits augment these benefits by two weeks when the unemployment rate is between 4.1 and 4.5 percent; they rise by two weeks for each additional one-half percentage point rise in the unemployment rate, up to a maximum of 32 weeks in regions where the unemployment rate is 11.5 percent. It should be noted that these regional extended benefits depend not on the location of employment but on the residence of the claimant; thus, the claimant can move to a high-unemployment region in order to extend his or her benefits.

Although the maximum UI entitlement is 50 weeks in a 52-week period, the generous regional extended benefits scheme seriously weakens the relationship between weeks of insured employment and weeks of benefits. In a region of unemployment in excess of 11.5 percent, for example, the availability of regional extended benefits means that 14 weeks of employment will generate 46 weeks of benefits — 14 from phase I and 32 from regional benefits. On the other hand, in a region where only two weeks of regional benefits are available, a worker who logs 52 weeks of employment (or 152 weeks, for that matter) qualifies for only 40 weeks of benefits — 25 under phase I, 13 under phase II, and two under regional benefits. It is obvious that this arrangement creates serious horizontal equity problems, since it treats otherwise identical workers differently because they were employed in different regions — or, more correctly, because they claimed benefits in different regions. The rationale for, and an evaluation of, these regional benefits appears below.

## Benefit Levels

The benefits themselves equal 60 percent of insurable earnings over the contribution period; in 1986, maximum insurable earnings were $495 per week. The tax-back rate on income earned while on benefit is 0 percent on the first 15 percent of the claimant's insurable earnings (or the first 25 percent of benefits) and 100 percent thereafter. These rates apply to each accounting period and not to the entire duration of the benefits. Unemployment contributions are tax deductible, and benefits are included in income for income tax purposes. High-income beneficiaries are subject to a special surtax of up to 30 percent of their benefits.

## Financing

Employers, employees, and the federal government all contribute to the financing of the UI program. The basic employee premium for 1986 was $2.35 for each $100 of weekly insurable earnings (up to the weekly maximum of $495). Emloyers contribute at 1.4 times this rate. In principle, the employer-employee premiums are designed to cover the costs of benefits for phases I and II and for the benefits relating to sickness, maternity leave, adoption, and work sharing. Administrative costs, including the National Employment Service, also come out of premiums.

The federal government absorbs the cost of regionally extended benefits, the benefits for self-employed fishermen, and the cost of extended benefits relating to any approved training or job creation projects.

In 1984, roughly 11 million Canadians were covered under UI. The number of UI claims terminating in that year totaled 2.6 million. Thus, UI claimants represent just under one-quarter of the covered population. This does not convert into 25 percent of covered individuals, however, since individuals can file more than one claim in a given year.

### The Pressures for Reform

Among the frequently cited concerns associated with the UI program — concerns that I share — are the following:

• It is becoming more and more a program that focuses on income distribution or redistribution goals, rather than on insurance goals, even though it is a particularly unsuitable instrument for tackling income redistribution.
• It violates horizontal equity principles by treating otherwise identical individuals differently because they work or reside in different places.
• It contributes to the high unemployment rate.
• It increases the duration of unemployment.
• It subsidizes and encourages persons with temporary and unstable employment patterns at the expense of longer-term employees.
• It subsidizes industries with unstable employment patterns at the expense of those with stable patterns.
• It inhibits the processes of economic adjustment within Canada.

This section discusses some of these concerns.

### UI and Income Distribution

There appears to be a growing trend to load all manner of social and income distribution policies on UI. In the summer of 1985, to cite a recent example, Employment Minister Flora MacDonald announced that forest fire fighters henceforth would be eligible for UI; they had been ineligible previously because of the short-term nature of their work. As UI embraces more features of social policy, both the rationale for the program and public support for it become more and more tenuous.

The problem is not that income distribution concerns are unimportant. Far from it. The problem is that UI is a very poor instrument for achieving income distribution goals. The Macdonald Commission noted:

[I]ncome redistribution does not constitute an appropriate application of the UI system. There are several reasons for this conclusion. Canadian income-distribution objectives focus on family income and need, while UI benefits are directed to the individual worker and are unrelated to other income or assets. In addition, the accounting period (the period over which benefits and income are reconciled) would have to be substantially lengthened, since the weekly accounting period presently in use is much shorter than that usually considered appropriate for income-support programs intended to reconcile income and needs. To change the UI system along these lines would be bound to interfere significantly with the program's social insurance objective which, in Commissioners' view, should be the primary focus of unemployment insurance.

This emphasis on the social insurance function of the UI program does not imply that this Commission opposes programs with redistributive objectives. On the contrary, our view is simply that unemployment insurance is an inappropriate means by which to attempt this important objective, and that explicit income-security programs are much more likely to be effective for this purpose.[2]

Table 9 presents some evidence relating to the income distribution implications of UI relative to other types of transfers. Over 60 percent of UI benefits go to the top three income quintiles, and 86 percent accrue to family units with incomes above Statistics Canada's low-income cutoff. Although these data are not corrected for the 30 percent tax-back rate on UI benefits, the fact remains that UI benefits are not well targeted to income distribution goals.

Under a pure insurance program, the income distribution implications of UI would be irrelevant. Under the present program, however, with its social and income distribution objectives, these concerns do become important. One obvious remedy for reform is to convert UI into a social insurance program and to use more appropriate instruments or programs to achieve the broader social objectives of the present UI scheme — such as maternity benefits, regional benefits, and benefits for self-employed fishermen. This remedy is the cornerstone of the reform proposals discussed later in this chapter.

## Industry Cross-Subsidization

UI subsidizes seasonal industries at the expense of more stable industries by encouraging layoffs rather than reductions in working hours.

---

[2]Canada, Royal Commission on the Economic Union and Development, Prospects for Canada, *Report*, vol. 2 (Ottawa: Supply and Services Canada, 1985), p. 602.

### Table 9
### *Transfer Payments, 1981*
### *(by quintile and income cutoff point)*

| Transfer payment | Quintile[a] | | | | | Low-income cutoff[b] | |
|---|---|---|---|---|---|---|---|
| | First (lowest) | Second | Third | Fourth | Fifth (highest) | Below | Above |
| Unemployment insurance[c] | 11.6 | 24.6 | 23.2 | 21.3 | 19.3 | 14.1 | 85.9 |
| Social assistance[d] | 61.0 | 22.8 | 7.6 | 4.8 | 4.8 | 67.5 | 32.5 |
| OAS/GIS[e] | 41.0 | 32.4 | 11.5 | 7.7 | 7.4 | 33.4 | 66.6 |
| CPP/QPP[f] | 23.3 | 35.4 | 17.9 | 13.1 | 10.3 | 18.8 | 81.2 |
| Family allowance[g] | 7.8 | 14.6 | 22.7 | 28.1 | 26.8 | 15.8 | 84.2 |
| Child tax credit[h] | 11.6 | 21.5 | 34.0 | 25.1 | 7.8 | 22.9 | 77.1 |
| Other transfers[i] | 1.7 | 26.7 | 23.3 | 15.5 | 14.8 | 22.2 | 77.8 |
| *All transfers[j]* | *29.1* | *27.4* | *17.2* | *14.1* | *12.2* | *28.6* | *71.4* |

[a]Income quintiles were computed using total money income and published cutoffs for 1981.

[b]1978 low-income cutoff updated to 1981.

[c]Includes sickness, maternity, retraining, and retirement benefits. Not corrected for 30 percent tax-back rate applicable in some cases.

[d]Received from provincial and municipal governments. Includes assistance to needy mothers with dependent children, to the blind and disabled, and income supplement programs.

[e]OAS, GIS, and spouse's allowance.

[f]Retirement pensions, survivors' benefits (widows, orphans), and disability pensions.

[g]Federal and provincial (Quebec, Alberta) allowances. Reported by the person claiming the child as a tax deduction.

[h]To be reported by the recipient of family allowances (usually the female parent).

[i]Includes veterans' pensions (veterans, widows, dependents) and other war allowances, worker's compensation, training allowances, various provincial grants, and tax credits.

[j]The sum of the seven transfers listed above.

Note: Statistics Canada warns that the coverage of Social assistance and Other transfers is lower than in other cases.

Source: François Vaillancourt, "Income Distribution and Economic Security in Canada: An Overview," in François Vaillancourt, ed., *Income Distribution and Economic Security in Canada*, Collected Research Studies of the Royal Commission on the Economic Union and Development Prospects for Canada no. 1 (Toronto: University of Toronto Press, 1985), Table 1-20.

## Table 10
### *Benefit-Contribution (Benefit-Cost) Ratios of Unemployment Insurance by Industry, 1977*

| Industry | Ratio > 1 | Ratio < 1 |
|---|---|---|
| Agriculture | 1.50 | |
| Forestry | 5.09 | |
| Fishing and hunting | 2.10 | |
| Construction | 2.46 | |
| Nondurable goods (food and beverages, etc.) | 1.24 | |
| Recreation (sports, tourism, etc.) | 1.67 | |
| Personal services | 1.40 | |
| Teaching | | 0.38 |
| Public services | | 0.15 |
| Communications | | 0.36 |
| Mining | | 0.67 |
| Finance, insurance, and real estate | | 0.75 |
| Retail trade | | 0.84 |
| Commercial services | | 0.91 |
| Transportation | | 0.58 |
| Durable goods | | 0.87 |
| *Total* | *1.00* | |

Source: Jean-Michel Cousineau, "Unemployment Insurance and Labour Market Adjustment," in François Vaillancourt, ed., *Income Distribution and Economic Security in Canada*, Collected Research Studies of the Royal Commission on the Economic Union and Development Prospects for Canada no. 1 (Toronto: University of Toronto Press, 1985), p. 206.

Moreover, because the benefit system is biased toward spells of short-term employment and because the premiums are not related to layoff patterns in seasonal industries, UI gives Canadians an incentive to seek employment in these industries — an incentive that would not exist under a scheme based more purely on insurance principles.

Table 10, which presents UI benefit-cost ratios by industry, illustrates this point. It is evident that substantial industry cross-subsidization exists — from industries such as public services and teaching to those such as construction and forestry. The problem is, of course, that UI contribution rates are everywhere the same, regardless of the industry or the pattern of layoffs. Numerous analysts have argued for "experience rating" — that is, the gearing of UI premiums to the likelihood or risk of layoffs.[3] Indeed, the Macdonald Commission asserts that it "views experience rating as the most important change that should be made to Canada's existing UI system."[4]

In dealing with the problem of industry cross-subsidization, a compromise of sorts is possible between introducing experience rating and reducing the bias in the present system toward rewarding short-term employment. A requirement of, say, three weeks of employment for each week of benefits also would reduce the benefit-cost ratios that favor seasonal industries and other industries with volatile layoff patterns.

## *Horizontal Equity*

The maximum benefit that a long-term employee can receive is 60 percent of his or her annual insurable earnings. If the employee resides in a very low unemployment area, where the maximum benefit period may be only 38 weeks, the maximum value of benefits will be only about 45 percent of annual insurable earnings. On the other hand, a claimant with ten weeks of employment who resides in a region of high unemployment can become eligible to receive as much as 240 percent of earnings.[5] This state of affairs is not only vividly inequitable but inefficient as well, since it tends to develop a "UI culture" in which employment for ten weeks and UI for the remainder of the year is an acceptable lifestyle.

Thus, both equity and efficiency considerations argue for reforms that would tilt UI benefits toward rewarding long-term, rather than short-term, labor force attachment.

## *UI and Economic Adjustment*

UI runs afoul of efficiency and economic adjustment concerns in several respects. First, it is generally conceded, and well documented, that the impact of the generous 1971 UI revisions has been to increase the overall Canadian unemployment rate: "The 1971 revisions of the Unemployment Insurance Act, which increased the generosity of the UI scheme in several respects, are generally considered to have increased unemployment by some 1 to 2 percentage points."[6] Part of this increase has resulted from

---

[3]See, for example, Jonathan R. Kesselman, *Financing Canadian Unemployment Insurance* (Toronto: Canadian Tax Foundation, 1983); Edward A. Carmichael, *Tackling the Federal Deficit*, Observation no. 26 (Toronto: C.D. Howe Institute, 1984); and Jean-Michel Cousineau, "Unemployment Insurance and Labour Market Adjustment," in François Vaillancourt, ed., *Income Distribution and Economic Security in Canada*, Collected Research Studies of the Royal Commission on the Economic Union and Development Prospects for Canada no. 1 (Toronto: University of Toronto Press, 1985).
[4]Macdonald Commission, *Report*, vol. 2, p. 611.
[5]Ibid., p. 612
[6]Ibid., p. 595.

the impact of UI benefits on the duration of unemployment. Estimates of increased duration range from 1.4 to 2.0 weeks.[7]

Second, the combination of the 1971 revisions and the generosity of regional benefits has dramatically affected internal migration within Canada. Following up on a study of my own, a very ambitious study by Winer and Gauthier finds that the impact of UI has been to discourage 8,000 people emigrating from Atlantic Canada each year, other things being equal.[8] By providing incentives for the unemployed to remain in relatively low employment areas, UI certainly does not contribute to the longer-term well-being of individual Canadians. To the extent that it is a goal to alleviate regional disparities, there are instruments for accomplishing this objective that are more appropriate than UI. The reform proposals later in the chapter focus on alternative approaches to meeting this objective.

Third, some aspects of UI have compounded existing adjustment problems.[9] The provision of UI benefits to self-employed fishermen, for example, has both increased the rate of unemployment in the Atlantic provinces and hampered the rationalization of the fishing industry. There are more fishermen, and fishing operations are smaller, than the economics of the industry would dictate. Suppose that Ottawa had granted the same privilege to self-employed farmers in Saskatchewan. There is little doubt that such an initiative would have altered dramatically the economic geography of that province. Saskatchewan now would have a considerably larger population, the farms would be smaller and less efficient, and, most likely, the incentive environment of that province would have been altered in a way that weakened its economic fabric. To be sure, Saskatchewan has gone through some tough times as its farms have become larger and more capitalized. Nonetheless, if efficiency is a criterion, Saskatchewan has good reason to be thankful that its farmers have not been treated in the same manner as have fishermen in Atlantic Canada.

It may well be that the fishing industry merits separate and special treatment. If so, it should not be difficult to design an intelligent support scheme that embodies both appropriate incentives and a rationalization of the industry. UI does neither.

---

[7]Ibid., p. 607.

[8]See Thomas J. Courchene, "Interprovincial Migration and Economic Adjustment," *Canadian Journal of Economics* 3 (1970): 550–576; and Stanley L. Winer and Denis Gauthier, *Internal Migration and Fiscal Structure: An Econometric Study of the Determinants of Interprovincial Migration in Canada* (Ottawa: Economic Council of Canada, 1982).

[9]The analysis in this paragraph is adapted from Thomas J. Courchene, "Avenues of Regional Adjustment: The Transfer System and Regional Disparities, in Michael Walker, ed., *Canadian Confederation at the Crossroads* (Vancouver: Fraser Institute, 1978), pp. 143–186.

## A Closer Look at Regional Benefits

At this juncture, it is instructive to focus in somewhat greater detail on the operations of the regional-benefits component of UI. When the program was revised in 1971, the federal government assumed the financial responsibility for both regional benefits and benefits that arose because of an increase in the national unemployment rate. In other words, the provision embodied both a regional component and a stabilization component. However, with the rather dramatic rise in the national unemployment rate in recent years, all but a few of the 48 regions defined for UI purposes now qualify for maximum regional benefits. In the present time frame, therefore, a call for curtailing regional benefits cannot be equated to depriving selected provinces of UI inflows. All provinces would be affected, albeit to varying degrees. Thus, what triggers the bulk of the regional benefits is no longer the differentiation in unemployment rates across regions but, rather, the high national unemployment rate. Or, to put the matter in terms of the original rationale, the stabilization or pump-priming goal has overtaken the regional goal. This being the case, there are ways in which the federal government can pursue employment creation or pump priming that are far better suited to the purpose than the UI program.

Moreover, the existence of regional benefits not only means, as I noted above, that ten-week claimants can receive benefits equal to roughly 2 1/2 times their earnings; it also provides a very substantial incentive not to work beyond the ten weeks. Consider the following example. Working from week one through week nine generates no UI benefits. The tenth week triggers 42 weeks of benefits — that is, benefits sufficient to carry the claimant right through to the next working season. If one focuses only on the calendar year, working beyond ten weeks generates very little net income for the worker. Assume that the worker is employed at or below the maximum insured earnings level (that is, $495 per week); the 60 percent UI benefit rate means the return from working for week 11 is only 40 percent of the weekly earnings, since the worker, in effect, is foregoing a week of benefits that would have equaled 60 percent of his or her weekly earnings. This 40 percent is subject not only to income tax but to UI premiums, CPP premiums, and, if applicable, union dues. Moreover, the fact that claimants can earn up to 25 percent of benefits without a reduction in UI provides a further incentive to file a claim after ten weeks of work. It is also likely that, in some areas, there will be community pressure on individuals to quit work or accept a layoff after ten weeks in order to provide work and, therefore, UI support, for other members of the community.

Although many Canadians may disapprove of such activities, it is

**Table 11**
*Modal Number of Benefit Weeks Claimed
by Weeks of Insured Employment, 1984*

| Weeks of insurable employment | Modal number of benefit weeks claimed | | | | |
|---|---|---|---|---|---|
| | Atlantic provinces | Quebec | Ontario | Prairies | B.C. |
| 10 – 19 | 30 – 39 | 30 – 39 | 30 – 39 | 30 – 39 | 40 – 49 |
| 20 – 29 | 20 – 29 | 20 – 29 | 20 – 29 | 20 – 29 | 20 – 29 |
| | | | | | 30 – 39 |
| 30 – 39 | 10 – 19 | 10 – 19 | 10 – 19 | 10 – 19 | 10 – 19 |
| 40 – 49 | 0 – 9 | 0 – 9 | 0 – 9 | 0 – 9 | 0 – 9 |
| 50+ | 40 – 49 | 0 – 9 | 0 – 9 | 0 – 9 | 40 – 49 |

Source: Canada, Commission of Inquiry on Unemployment Insurance (Forget Commission), *Report* (Ottawa: Supply and Services Canada, 1986), Tables G3–G7.

important to emphasize that this behavior is entirely rational. The problem lies with the incentives embodied in the UI system and not with the individuals who decide to take advantage of the incentives. The next section presents a series of tables relating to the operations of UI that, in part at least, demonstrate that the provisions embodied in the UI program probably do have a substantial influence on the general pattern of benefits.

## The Relationship between Weeks Worked and Weeks Claimed

Tables 11, 12, and 13, compiled from Appendix G of the Forget Commission's *Report*, provide a convenient statistical summary of many of the concerns raised above. Table 11 indicates, for each region, the modal number of benefit weeks claimed, classified by number of weeks of prior insurable earnings. Consider the Atlantic region. For individuals who have between 10 and 19 weeks of insurable earnings before filing a claim, the following is the distribution of weeks and benefits: 4.2 percent of individuals claim benefits for 0–9 weeks, 8.4 percent for 10–19 weeks, 14.6 percent for 20–29 weeks, 43.1 percent for 30–39 weeks, 27.8 percent for 40–49 weeks, and 1.9 percent for 50+ weeks. Since the mode of the distribution is 30–39 weeks — that is, 43.1 percent — the 30–39 figure appears in Table 11.

What is revealing about these data is that modal weeks of benefits are inversely correlated with weeks of insured earnings prior to claims: those with 10–19 weeks of insured employment tend to claim 30–39 weeks of benefits, whereas those with 30–39 weeks of insurable employment tend to claim benefits for only 0–9 weeks.[10] More striking is the fact that this

[10]Note that these data relate to claims terminating in 1984. The claims may have originated in the previous year.

### Table 12
### *Distribution of Unemployment Insurance*
### *Claimants by Region and Weeks Worked, 1984*

| Weeks of insurable employment | Percent of claimants | | | | |
| --- | --- | --- | --- | --- | --- |
| | Atlantic provinces | Quebec | Ontario | Prairies | B.C. |
| 10 – 19 | 34.7 | 21.9 | 14.0 | 10.4 | 18.7 |
| 20 – 29 | 24.5 | 30.7 | 26.7 | 28.9 | 25.8 |
| 30 – 39 | 15.1 | 14.9 | 17.5 | 18.8 | 14.9 |
| 40 – 49 | 10.1 | 14.2 | 18.2 | 19.7 | 18.9 |
| 50 + | 15.6 | 18.3 | 23.6 | 23.2 | 21.8 |
| | 100.0 | 100.0 | 100.0 | 100.0 | 100.0 |

Source: Canada, Commission of Inquiry on Unemployment Insurance (Forget Commission), *Report* (Ottawa: Supply and Services Canada, 1986), Tables G3–G7.

pattern holds for all regions. To be sure, it probably is the case that individuals with longer labor force attachment prior to filing a claim are likely to be the higher skilled and, therefore, more likely to find reemployment. It is difficult, however, to escape the conclusion that the UI system and the incentives in UI are largely responsible for generating this relationship between weeks worked and weeks claimed.

While these patterns hold for all regions, there are also important differences between the regions. Table 12, which focuses on the distribution of claimants by region and by weeks worked, shows that in the Atlantic region a far larger percentage of UI claims arises from individuals with only 10–19 weeks of insured earnings while a smaller proportion arises from long-term labor force attachment (50+ weeks). Table 13 extends the geographical comparisons to the provincial level. Column 1 of that table presents "claimant rates", the ratio of claimants to contributions. These data are corrected for any multiple claims in 1984 by individuals. Thus, 57.7 percent of individuals in Newfoundland contributing to UI applied for or were receiving UI benefits in 1984. The five eastern provinces plus British Columbia experienced claimant rates above the 28 percent national average. The last three columns of Table 13 focus on UI benefit-cost ratios. While the earlier analysis suggested that UI benefits were not particularly well targeted with respect to the income distribution characteristics of the recipients, the data in these last three columns reveal that, except for British Columbia, it is the "have-not", or equalization-receiving, provinces that receive more in benefits than they contribute in premiums. This is only to be expected, and it is a desirable feature of any unemployment insurance program.

Thus, these data appear to indicate that the incentives in the UI program do influence the pattern of benefits. They also reveal, however, that

## Table 13
### *Benefit Rates and Income Transfers, 1984*

|  | Claimants as a percent of contributors | Total regular benefits ($ millions) | Ratio of benefits to contributions[a] | Excess of benefits over contributions ($ millions) |
|---|---|---|---|---|
|  | (1) | (2) | (3) | (4) |
| Newfoundland | 57.7 | 494 | 3.38 | 348 |
| Prince Edward Island | 49.7 | 93 | 2.83 | 60 |
| Nova Scotia | 35.6 | 403 | 1.40 | 115 |
| New Brunswick | 42.8 | 480 | 2.24 | 266 |
| Quebec | 33.5 | 2,945 | 1.24 | 578 |
| Ontario | 21.2 | 2,649 | 0.67 | − 1,323 |
| Manitoba | 24.8 | 299 | 0.78 | − 85 |
| Saskatchewan | 23.9 | 235 | 0.74 | − 83 |
| Alberta | 24.6 | 897 | 0.88 | − 122 |
| British Columbia | 33.3 | 1,376 | 1.22 | 248 |
| *Canada* | *28.0* | *9,905* | *1.00* | *0* |

[a]The federal contribution is apportioned using the distribution of federal tax revenue.

Sources: Column 1 is from Statistics Canada, *Benefit Periods Established and Terminated under the Unemployment Insurance Act, 1984*, Cat. no. 73-201, 1986. The remaining three columns are from Canada, Commission of Inquiry on Unemployment Insurance (Forget Commission), *Report* (Ottawa: Supply and Services Canada, 1986), Table G12.

UI plays a key role in the economic life of many of the poorer provinces. Taken together, they suggest that policymakers have to be very careful when making recommendations for UI reform. In particular, three concerns appear uppermost. The first is simply a repetition of a point made earlier, namely, that problems relating to UI must not be viewed as reflecting in any way on the character or behavior of the claimants. Claimants respond rationally and legitimately to the set of perverse incentives embodied in the UI legislation. Second, any changes in UI have to be introduced gradually. Third, and relatedly, reform measures probably will have to incorporate some *quid pro quo* in terms of, say, job creation programs, given the importance of UI in the economies of a number of provinces.

To conclude this section relating to the pressures for UI reform, it may be instructive to focus on the assessment of the UI program in Newfoundland contained in the report of a Royal Commission in that province.[11]

---

[11]Newfoundland, Royal Commission on Employment and Unemployment, *Building On Our Strengths* (St. John's: Queen's Printer, 1986).

## *The Newfoundland Royal Commission*

Among the many serious problems that the Newfoundland Royal Commission associates with the operations of UI are the following:

(i) *The system undermines the intrinsic value of work.*
'Fishing for stamps' or 'working for stamps' detracts from the intrinsic value of work itself. Work is no longer a craft where the artisan takes pride in the skill of the operation and the quality of the good or service produced. It is merely a means to an end.

(ii) *The system undermines good working habits and discipline.*
When one knows that one's work is meaningless — epitomized by local stereotypes of yet another community wharf or yet another fence around the cemetery — there seems little point in working hard, turning up on time, putting in a full day's work or worrying about the quality of what is produced....

(iii) *The system undermines the importance of education.*
Little or no qualifications are required to become an inshore fisherman, a fish-plant worker or a construction worker, or to be employed on a short-term make-work project. It is as easy to get the 10 weeks' work to qualify for UI with a Grade 8 education as it is with a university degree — at least, that is the local perception. Hence, there is little incentive to get a better education for the work world. In addition, the UI system actually penalizes people for aspiring to further their education by cutting off their benefits if they become full-time students.

(iv) *UI is a disincentive to work.*
Once one qualifies for UI in outport Newfoundland, one's basic security is assured. It would be folly to threaten this security by actions that would disqualify one from receiving benefits. But UI regulations require the reporting of all earned income, and benefits can be discontinued if earned income exceeds 25 per cent of benefits. Furthermore, one must remain available for work, even in situations where few labour-market opportunitites exist. It is *safer* to do nothing than to work.

(v) *UI undermines personal and community initiatives.*
Related to the last point, but worthy of comment in its own right, is the extent to which the 'ten-week syndrome' undermines the traditional economic adaptations of many Newfoundlanders. To practice occupational pluralism — for example, by doing some logging for the local sawmill in the fall, following 10 weeks on a make-work project — is to jeopardize one's UI status....

(vi) *UI discourages self employment and small-scale enterprise.*
The UI system has various deleterious effects upon local enterprise. Seasonal fish-plant operators have had to adapt to the 'ten-week syndrome' by hiring many more plant workers during the season than would otherwise be needed. Workers expect to get laid off to give someone else a chance once they get their 10 stamps. This is a rational adaptation from the point of view of the community: it shares out the available work, qualifies the maximum number of people for income stabilization payments (UI benefits) during the off-season and thereby maximizes both household and community incomes. For the fish-plant operator, however, it means higher operating costs due to labour turnover, lower productivity and difficulties in finding workers during the fall and winter; plant operators also find that it is difficult to get fishermen to continue supplying fish plants in the fall, once they have qualified for UI....

(vii) *The UI make-work system encourages political patronage.*
MHAs and MPs are in a good position to bring wider perspectives and comparative experiences from elsewhere to bear upon local problems, and to make real contributions to long-term development and employment enhancement, but this potential is being undermined by the present UI make-work system.

(viii) *UI make-work distorts the efforts of local development groups.*
[T]he role that they should be playing as agents of long-term economic development is distorted by their role in the UI make-work system....

(xi) *The system is vulnerable to manipulation.*
The UI system is similar to the tax system in that its myriad rules and regulations confront its users with strategic choices as to how to maximize personal financial benefit. Just as the business person or professional has become adept at playing the tax system, so the seasonal worker has become adept at playing the UI system. The morality is the same in both cases. The Commission was told about many tactics designed to manipulate the UI system, many of them displaying a degree of ingenuity that would be the envy of the best tax lawyer. Many Newfoundlanders express concern about UI manipulation, such as:

- job rotation, where all of the work-force in an area is rotated through the available jobs so its members qualify for benefits;
- employers submitting records for higher salaries than they are paying the employees so that there will be no reduction in income when the employees are laid off;
- employers having employees on the payroll for 10- or 20-week periods but not actually paying them, just making the necessary

remittances to the Receiver General and preparing a record of employment;
- employees working while they are receiving benefits but not recording this work;
- individuals setting up incorporated companies for the sole purpose of having an employer who can deduct UI premiums to enable them to qualify for benefits. If an individual owns less than 40 per cent of a company, then he/she can legitimately be on the payroll;
- Social Services providing short-term employment for recipients of their benefits so that the burden of caring for these people is shifted from the provincial to the federal government.[12]

Following this litany of concerns, the Commission notes that "while it would be socially unacceptable, economically disastrous and politically suicidal simply to cut back drastically on UI payments to Newfoundlanders without providing alternative income support and income supplementation,"[13] it is eminently possible to undertake a redesign of the entire income security system. Such an ideal system would be designed to provide (a) *income support* for those that have no form of earned income; (b) *income supplementation* for those whose earned income is so low that it precludes their enjoying a decent standard of living; and (c) *income maintenance* — for example, UI, workers' compensation. Again, in the words of the Commission:

> The overall system should be changed to accord better with the three functions it fulfills. For income support, a Guaranteed Basic Income system for households should be implemented, supplemented by Social Assistance benefits for households without any earnings. For income supplementation, an Earned Income Supplementation scheme for either households or individuals should be created. To avoid having to apply to government officials for assistance, these two schemes should be administered through the income tax system. UI would then revert to its intended function of providing income maintenance for people in transition between permanent jobs or on short-term lay-off, sick leave or maternity leave. The revised income security system should also include incentives for people to further their education and training.[14]

The Commission offers the following overall recommendation:

---

[12]Ibid., pp. 406–410.
[13]Ibid., p. 417.
[14]Ibid.

> The Government of Newfoundland and Labrador should enter into negotiations with the Government of Canada for the implementation of a new income security system along the lines suggested in this Report, possibly using Newfoundland as a pilot project for Canada as a whole.[15]

While the thrust of the present study is that the time is not yet ripe for this sort of "big bang" approach to the income security area, the situation in Newfoundland with both regionally extended and fishing benefits playing dominant roles is such that the province may well be the place to experiment with comprehensive income security approaches.

I turn now to my own, less grandiose, approach to UI reform.

## *The Approach to Reform*

In the matter of UI reform, the claims of efficiency, adjustment, equity, and even regional development would all appear to point to the same conclusion: return the system to social insurance principles and spin off the various socio-economic goals currently associated with UI to other, more appropriate programs. What is not so apparent is how this reform can be accomplished, since it represents a rather dramatic alteration of the status quo. UI is closely intertwined with several other programs; any reform of UI must extend to the subsystem as a whole. Therefore, the approach to reform outlined in the remainder of this chapter focuses on both the UI program itself and the other components of the subsystem. Chapter 11 will integrate these proposals even more fully into the overall subsystem reform package.

### *Returning UI to Insurance Principles*

The following reforms would be consistent with reintroducing a greater reliance on social insurance principles as well as an improved incentive structure in the design of UI:

• Separate from UI the many income support and socio-economic programs that have accreted to it, such as the regional benefits component and the benefits for self-employed fishermen. Since these components are currently funded by the federal government, transferring them to other programs or departments should not be difficult. The benefits for fishermen, for example, might fall naturally to the Department of Regional Industrial Expansion (DRIE), at least temporarily — collaborating with the appropriate provincial counterparts — and some of the funds currently

---

[15]Ibid., p. 416.

used for regional extended benefits probably should be diverted to job creation programs that would be directed, initially at least, to those areas that currently receive the regional benefits.

• The minimum entrance requirement in terms of weeks worked should increase to, say, at least 15 weeks, and this requirement should apply uniformly across the country.

• The duration of benefits should be more closely related to weeks of employment. The following illustrates what I have in mind:

> — For the first 25 weeks, one week of employment would qualify a claimant for one week of benefits.
> — From week 26 to week 51, two weeks of employment would be required to earn one week of benefits.
> — Beyond 51 weeks, three weeks of employment would be required to earn one week of benefits. The maximum benefit period would be 52 weeks. Hence, under the above requirements, which would have to be introduced gradually, an individual would have to work for 93 weeks in order to qualify for the full 52 weeks of benefit.[16]

• The weekly benefit should be lowered to 50 percent of the average of the claimant's best 15 weeks of insured earnings during the qualifying period. However, UI beneficiaries should be able to engage in part-time or temporary work while on claim. The tax-back rate on income earned while on claim should also be 50 percent, so that if in any given settlement period — defined to be no shorter than one month — a beneficiary earns an income equal to previous insurable earnings, he or she will receive no UI benefits. This 50 percent claw-back of benefits is likely to be far more conducive to reentry into the labor force than the current 0 percent on the first 25 percent of benefits and 100 percent on the remainder.

• Experience rating should be introduced if it can be done in an administratively and economically feasible manner. It should be noted, however, that much of the interindustry subsidization under UI arises because short-term labor force attachment is so highly rewarded under the current UI benefits structure. Under the present proposal, experience rating, while still desirable, is not indispensable.

• Since even apart from the removal of regional and fishing benefits this program would likely generate lower benefits, the premiums could be scaled down. However, there is alternative that may have some merit. A growing number of very long term employees are finding themselves unemployed, often because their skills have become obsolete. Without some

---

[16]Note that the provisions relating to the first 25 weeks and also to weeks 26–51 replicate the first two phases of the existing provisions. Phase III — regionally extended benefits — is reduced (gradually) by the provisions relating to weeks 52–93.

education, retraining, or mobility, their reemployment prospects may be bleak. It would be consistent with social insurance principles to alter UI to accommodate these very long term workers. For example, beyond the initial 93 qualifying weeks for full coverage, employees could be allowed to accumulate either more weeks or a higher percentage of insurable earnings for each further year of employment. Some caution would have to be exercised to ensure that these long-term benefits went only to claimants who were willing to undertake skill enhancement activities. This aspect of a reformed UI system would have some of the overtones of the Macdonald Commission's proposed "Transitional Adjustment Assistance Program" (TAAP). I shall develop the idea further in Chapter 11.

• Both labor and management should have more say in the actual running of the UI program, since they would now be responsible, through their premiums, for the entire funding of the program.

• An annual adjustment in premiums to match benefits would lead to a procyclical policy of raising premium rates during periods of economic downswing. The UI system should either have access to the consolidated revenue fund or the ability to float its own debt so that premiums and benefits could be reconciled over the cycle, rather than on an annual basis.

This approach to redesigning UI would still favor short-term labor attachment to some extent. Horizontal equity, however, now would prevail in the sense that entrance requirements and benefit levels would be uniform for employees with identical employment experience, regardless of location. Moreover, it would no longer be possible, as it is now, for claimants to receive benefits in excess of their insured earnings. The new system would reduce substantially the incentives for short-term labor force attachment and enhance the incentives for reemployment. Finally, some of the funds — initially, perhaps, all of the funds — previously devoted to regional benefits would be available for new job creation or skill enhancement programs in the regions affected. In terms of income redistribution, human capital enhancement, and regional development, this surely represents a preferable allocation of spending.

## Implications for the Subsystem

Although a reorientation of UI toward insurance principles would incorporate substantially improved incentives across a broad range of fronts, reform on this scale probably is not possible, politically or even in terms of economic considerations, without a series of accommodations. First of all, the reforms could not be introduced in one fell swoop. A phase-in period would be necessary.

Second, the shedding of the various noninsurance features of UI — features that provide income support rather than income replacement — would cause transitional problems both for regions and individuals. Surprisingly, the elimination of coverage for self-employed fishermen probably would be the easiest change to accommodate. The dollar value of the existing benefits simply could be transferred to another federal department, such as DRIE, and appropriately labeled as an "income support" or "income supplementation" program for fishermen. One would expect, however, that the long-term goal of the program would be to rationalize the operations of the fishing industry. Indeed, it may be possible to mount a negative income tax system for fishermen. One could follow, in fact, the recommendation of the Newfoundland Royal Commission and use that province as a pilot project for developing a full-blown GAI. In this case, the savings from regionally extended benefits and fishing benefits would be diverted to the GAI.

Short of the GAI alternative, the elimination of regional benefits would raise more serious difficulties. For one thing, aggregate demand in the affected regions would fall. This problem could be addressed, initially, through job creation and skill enhancement activities directed to these regions and individuals. Over the longer term, however, these activities presumably would have to be justified on economic or regional development grounds or else be phased out gradually. In addition, the lessened duration of UI benefits for short-term workers under the above proposal might result in a temporary increase in the number of UI exhaustees who are forced to resort to provincial welfare. Although the available evidence suggests that, under the current system, only about 10 percent of exhaustees turn immediately to welfare,[17] the number might still be large enough to strain severely the fiscal positions of the affected provinces. Again, transitional and, probably, some permanent accommodations would be necessary. Some approaches toward this end are outlined in later chapters.

The essential point is that without transitional and, perhaps, some permanent compensatory initiatives, there is little likelihood of a meaningful UI reform. Canadians should welcome such compensatory initiatives, not only because they would facilitate much-needed reform of the core of the UI program, but also because UI is a woefully inadequate vehicle for achieving these noninsurance objectives.

---

[17]About one-third of the exhaustees obtain employment after they run out of benefits, and about 60 percent of them belong to households in which another member is employed. See Canada, Department of Employment and Immigration, *UI Exhaustee Study* (Ottawa: Supply and Services Canada, 1982).

# 8

# *The Canada Assistance Plan*

## *The Status Quo*

The Canada Assistance Plan (CAP) has two main components — social assistance (welfare) and social services. Both components are under provincial control, with the costs shared by Ottawa on a 50-50 basis. As Table 2 (in Chapter 3) indicates, the federal outlays for CAP for fiscal year 1986–87 were expected to be $4.059 billion. The level of welfare assistance is determined provincially and varies substantially across the provinces. As the first column of Table 14 shows, the annual welfare levels for a family of four — two adults and two children — range from $12,720 in Saskatchewan to $6,900 in New Brunswick. The second column provides one measure of each province's welfare "needs", namely, the ratio of welfare recipients to population. Not surprisingly, the five eastern provinces have the largest welfare burdens, in some cases, they are twice as large as those of the other provinces.

An obvious consequence of the 50-50 cost-sharing formula is that the federal contribution to social assistance has less to do with a province's "needs" than with the province's own chosen level of per capita expenditure on social assistance. Column 3 of Table 14 presents the value of overall CAP transfers per capita; the data in column 4 refer only to the welfare components of the federal transfers. The latter figures range from $121 per capita in New Brunswick to $46 per capita in Manitoba.

There are several reasons why provincial per capita welfare expenditures — and, therefore, federal expenditures as well — vary so widely. For one thing, some provinces have more resources than others. For another, the perception of what constitutes an adequate level of welfare payments is bound to vary from province to province. Another, rather less obvious, cause of the variation in expenditures is the variation across provinces in the family composition of welfare recipients. British Columbia's spending on welfare (column 4) is high, in part because a relatively large proportion of the welfare recipients in that province are unattached individuals (column 5). Payments to unattached individuals amount, in general, to far more than one-quarter of the payments to a family of four. Finally, the application of the "needs test" across the provinces can and does vary considerably. In Quebec, for example, checks by "welfare inspectors" have revealed that about 20 percent of family units currently

## Table 14
### *Operations of the Canada Assistance Plan*

|  | 1983 welfare levels[a] ($) | Welfare recipients as a % of population[b] (1982) | Federal CAP spending per capita ($) | Federal spending on social assistance (1982–83) | Unattached recipients as a % of total (1977–78) |
|---|---|---|---|---|---|
|  | (1) | (2) | (3) | (4) | (5) |
| Newfoundland | 7,752 | 9.6 | 116 | 69 | 43 |
| P.E.I. | 10,380 | 9.2 | 149 | 92 | 50 |
| Nova Scotia | 9,984 | 7.6 | 101 | 70 | 45 |
| New Brunswick | 6,900 | 9.0 | 154 | 121 | 45 |
| Quebec | 8,800 | 8.7 | 180 | 115 | 59 |
| Ontario | 8,004 | 4.7 | 85 | 60 | 42 |
| Manitoba | 11,184 | 4.6 | 89 | 46 | 44 |
| Saskatchewan | 12,720 | 4.9 | 122 | 67 | 52 |
| Alberta | 12,432 | 4.0 | 132 | 79 | 39 |
| British Columbia | 10,440 | 5.2 | 170 | 114 | 63 |
| *Canada* | *8,217* | *6.1* | *130* | *85* | *52* |

[a]Annual amount for two adults, two children.
[b]Recipients include dependents in any household receiving welfare.

Sources: Column 1 is from François Vaillancourt, "Income Distribution and Economic Security in Canada: An Overview," in François Vaillancourt, ed., *Income Distribution and Economic Security in Canada*, Collected Research Studies of the Royal Commission on the Economic Union and Development Prospects for Canada no. 1 (Toronto: University of Toronto Press, 1985), p. 40; columns 2–5 are from Adil Sayeed, "The Canada Assistance Plan: Some Background," in Thomas J. Courchene, David W. Conklin, and Gail C.A. Cook, eds., *Ottawa and the Provinces: The Distribution of Money and Power*, vol. 2 (Toronto: Ontario Economic Council, 1985), pp. 279–290.

receiving welfare do not, in fact, qualify for benefits or, at least, do not qualify for the level of benefits that they currently receive. One can be fairly confident that Quebec will enhance its procedures for screening welfare applicants. Other provinces may well follow.

Saskatchewan, Quebec, Manitoba, and Ontario have programs designed to supplement the income of the working poor. The role of these programs is to ensure that the income of the working poor is above that of welfare recipients in similar family circumstances. Each of the four provinces reduces the income supplement if income exceeds a given level — a reduction of one dollar for each two dollars of income in Saskatchewan and Ontario, one for three in Quebec, and one for four in Manitoba.[1] Programs for the working poor generally do not qualify for federal support under CAP — and, therefore, do not appear in the figures in column 4 of Table 14. In some cases, however, *ad hoc* agreements with Ottawa have been negotiated.

## Welfare: The Pressures for Reform

### Poverty Traps

There is a growing concern that the present income support, income replacement system is generating poverty traps; more and more able-to-work individuals and families appear to be drawn to welfare. To be sure, the 1982–84 recession likely was responsible in large part for forcing family units to resort to welfare in the first instance. But there is mounting evidence that the system itself is providing a major disincentive for these family units to reenter the work force.

Surprisingly, there has been very little research in this critical area. The major recent exception is an impressive Quebec government White Paper.[2] Table 15, reproduced from the White Paper, presents data that documents the degree to which the able-to-work have been resorting, or have been forced to resort, to the welfare system. During the 1973–83 period, the unable-to-work group of welfare recipients increased by 28 percent, whereas able-to-work recipients increased by 282 percent. As the White Paper notes:

> This high rate of growth [of able-to-work recipients] may be attributed to a number of factors: tighter labour market, stricter eligibility conditions for unemployment insurance, marked growth in the labour force, a different attitude towards work, and so on. The contribution of each of these factors is difficult to assess. What is certain, however, is that Québec does not have the means to allow this rapid growth to continue indefinitely.[3]

Nor, for that matter, do the other provinces.

---

[1]François Vaillancourt, "Income Distribution and Economic Security in Canada: An Overview," in François Vaillancourt, ed., *Income Distribution and Economic Security in Canada*, Collected Research Studies of the Royal Commission on the Economic Union and Development Prospects for Canada no. 1 (Toronto: University of Toronto Press, 1985), p. 41.
[2]Québec, Ministère des Finances, *White Paper on the Personal Tax and Transfer Systems* (Québec, 1984).
[3]Ibid., p. 124.

**Table 15**
*Social Aid Recipients in Quebec, 1973–83*

| | Able to work | | Unable to work | | Total | | Proportion of those able to work | Single persons | Families | Proportion of single persons |
|---|---|---|---|---|---|---|---|---|---|---|
| | No. | Percent change | No. | Percent change | No. | Percent change | | | | |
| 1973 | 69,196 | — | 108,176 | — | 177,372 | — | 39.2% | 94,203 | 83,169 | 53.1% |
| 1974 | 75,826 | 9.6% | 114,778 | 6.1% | 190,604 | 7.5% | 39.8 | 102,593 | 88,011 | 53.8 |
| 1975[a] | 85,996 | 13.4 | 121,204 | 5.6 | 207,200 | 8.7 | 41.5 | 117,905 | 89,295 | 56.9 |
| 1976 | 101,956 | 18.6 | 126,588 | 4.4 | 228,544 | 10.3 | 44.6 | 133,470 | 95,074 | 58.5 |
| 1977 | 114,853 | 12.6 | 126,152 | (0.3) | 241,005 | 5.4 | 47.7 | 142,769 | 98,236 | 59.2 |
| 1978 | 126,101 | 9.8 | 124,211 | (1.5) | 250,312 | 3.9 | 50.4 | 148,712 | 101,600 | 59.4 |
| 1979 | 142,472 | 13.0 | 128,408 | 3.4 | 270,880 | 8.2 | 52.6 | 163,817 | 107,063 | 60.5 |
| 1980 | 156,729 | 10.0 | 133,289 | 3.8 | 290,018 | 7.1 | 54.0 | 177,735 | 112,283 | 61.3 |
| 1981 | 174,395 | 11.3 | 134,896 | 1.2 | 309,291 | 6.6 | 56.4 | 192,225 | 117,066 | 62.2 |
| 1982 | 234,432 | 34.4 | 137,188 | 1.7 | 371,620 | 20.1 | 63.1 | 235,503 | 136,117 | 63.3 |
| 1983 | 264,180 | 12.7 | 138,690 | 1.1 | 402,870 | 8.4 | 65.6 | 254,810 | 148,060 | 63.3 |

[a]After 1975, households 65 and over (pensioners) were added prorata to clients classified as able or unable to work. The number varied between 3,000 and 5,000 during the 1975–83 period.

Source: Québec, Ministère des Finances, *White Paper on the Personal Income Tax and Transfer Systems* (Québec, 1984), p. 125.

One of the principal concerns of the Quebec White Paper is that the *overall* rate of taxation implicit in the transition from welfare to work is far too high. Table 16, also reproduced from the White Paper, sets out sample tax rates for a family of two that reenters the work force. Work that pays $4.00 per hour (the minimum wage in Quebec at that time) generates an average tax rate of 79 percent. This rate decreases to 69 percent for work at $7.50 per hour and to 60 percent at $10.75 per hour, but it is still very substantial. As I noted above, however, the Quebec welfare system, unlike those in most of the other provinces, allows low-income workers to retain some social assistance benefits — for example, the table shows that a worker whose wage is $4.00 per hour is eligible for annual "social aid" of $2,087. Without such a provision, the tax rate would be confiscatory.

What is more important, Table 16 neglects the range of other benefits to which welfare recipients may have access, including low-rental housing, drug and medicare plans, and loans and grants for postsecondary students. All told, the net impact of the move from welfare to work in Quebec could easily entail a 100 percent — that is, a fully confiscatory — tax rate. In several other provinces, the tax rate almost surely is well above 100 percent. Figure 1 presents some relevant data for a single-parent family living in Toronto. Marginal tax rates fluctuate considerably, but generally range from 75 to 100 percent for earned incomes up to $16,000, at which point the taxation of the family unit merges with the personal income tax rate structure. Finally, as the Quebec White Paper points out, any implicit income that a welfare recipient obtains from "domestic" production — the substitution of one's own labor for labor normally purchased in the market — and from barter or "underground" economy activities is also likely to decrease in the transition from welfare to work.

It is clear, then, that even in the face of a strong work ethic, the incentives to remain on welfare are also very strong. Confiscatory tax rates create a "veritable 'poverty wall' that encourages low income households to remain dependent on social assistance programs: this is the 'poverty trap'."[4] The recognition on the part of the working poor that they may be better off financially on welfare is a concern that ought to weigh heavily on all policymakers, federal and provincial.

Not surprisingly, the Quebec White Paper embodies recommendations that are designed to offset these perverse incentives. One general objective of the proposed reforms is to provide greater incentives for those currently on welfare to return to the labor market. For those welfare recipients who are unable to work, the system would continue to operate much as it currently does. Social assistance recipients who are able

---

[4]Bernard Fortin, "Income Security in Canada," in Vaillancourt, ed., *Income Distribution and Economic Security in Canada*, p. 169.

### Table 16
### *Method of Calculating Interest in Participating in the Labor Market*[a]
*(in dollars)*

| | No employ- ment income | At the minimum wage $4.00/hr. | At an interme- diate wage $7.50/hr. | At the average industrial wage $10.75/hr. |
|---|---|---|---|---|
| Gross employment income for 2,000 hours | — | 8,000 | 15,000 | 21,500 |
| Social aid | 8,807 | 2,087 | — | — |
| Employment income supplement | — | 685 | 119 | — |
| Taxes[a] | 2,134 | 1,868 | 445 | − 2,025 |
| Disposable income | 10,941 | 12,640 | 15,564 | 19,475 |
| Net earnings[c] | — | 1,699 | 4,623 | 8,534 |
| Net hourly wage increase (net earnings/2,000 hrs.) | — | 0.85/hr. | 2.31/hr. | 4.27/hr. |
| Government's share of the increase in income: Gross hourly employment income less net hourly wage increase | — | 3.15/hr. | 5.19/hr. | 6.48/hr. |
| *Implicit marginal tax rate* | | *79%* | *69%* | *60%* |

[a]Head of a two-parent family with two children under 6.

[b]Taxes include:

| | | | | |
|---|---|---|---|---|
| • Income tax and contributions to QPP | — | − 296 | − 1,688 | − 4,110 |
| • Family allowances, availability allowance, and child tax credit | 1,929 | 1,929 | 1,929 | 1,929 |
| • Property tax refund | 205 | 235 | 204 | 156 |
| *Total* | *2,134* | *1,868* | *445* | *− 2,025* |

[c]Change in disposable income compared with no employment income.

Source: Québec, Ministère des Finances, *White Paper on the Personal Income Tax and Transfer Systems* (Québec, 1984), p. 143.

87

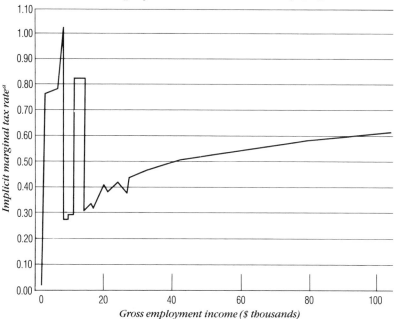

**Figure 1**
*Marginal Tax Rate by Level of*
*Employment Income in Toronto, 1983*

[a]Head of a single-parent family working 25 hours per week, 52 weeks per year, two children under six years of age, one child in day care, rent $3,600 per year.

Source: Bernard Fortin, "Income Security in Canada," in François Vaillancourt, ed., *Income Distribution and Economic Security in Canada,* Collected Research Studies of the Royal Commission on the Economic Union and Development Prospects for Canada no. 1 (Toronto: University of Toronto Press. 1985), p. 169.

to work, however, would be able to increase their benefits by taking part in programs designed to encourage their integration into the labor market, such as community work, industrial training, or a return to school. The goal would be to reduce to 50 percent the maximum overall marginal tax rate in the transition from welfare to work.

Another critical objective of the overall reform proposal is the integration, in terms of both design and administration, of the various tax, transfer, and expenditure programs directed to low-income Quebecers. The tax transfer system would be the principal delivery mechanism, and the welfare and tax system would be integrated to the extent that persons in receipt of benefits would not be subject to a positive tax, and vice versa.

Integration on the administrative side is just as important. In 1983, a Quebec couple that received social aid and that had a child under six was entitled to transfers totaling $1,562 for the essential needs of the child. However, as the Introductory Paper of the White Paper notes:

> This amount is spread over 5 different programs and is paid by 5 different agencies or departments: a supplementary benefit paid by the ministère de la Main-d'oeuvre et de la Securité du revenu..., an availability allowance paid by the ministère du Revenu du Québec..., a family allowance paid by the Québec Pension Plan..., a family allowance paid by the federal Department of Health and Welfare..., and the federal child tax credit paid by Revenue Canada.[5]

The White Paper considers several alternative schemes designed to achieve its general objectives, using numerical general equilibrium analysis to evaluate them. Under what the technical background supplement to the White Paper terms "average" labor supply elasticities, the welfare reforms — which amount to a guaranteed annual income scheme — would generate between 18,000 and 67,000 new full-time jobs for Quebec, depending on the particular reform alternative.[6] These figures become much larger if one assumes that a reduction in marginal tax rates in the transition from welfare to work would increase labor supply elasticities.

What is pathbreaking about these results is that they represent one of the first attempts to assess the *economic* impact of the perverse (antiwork) incentives that characterize most, if not all, provincial social assistance programs.

The greatest and most obvious problem with the welfare work subsystem is that it serves as a poverty trap — the returns to reentering the work force are low and often negative. Indeed, the evidence cited in the Quebec White Paper suggests that some of the working poor are simply throwing in the towel, to join the ranks of welfare recipients because they cannot significantly improve their living standards by going to work. It seems self-evident that Canada simply can no longer tolerate, on economic or social policy grounds, a system that embodies such incentives.

Finally, before I move on to other concerns relating to the operation of the welfare system, it is instructive to note that the recipients of UI

[5]Québec, Ministère des Finances, *White Paper on the Personal and Tax and Transfer Systems: Introductory Paper* (Québec, 1984), p. 18.
[6]Bernard Fortin and Henri-Paul Rousseau, *Economic Evaluation of the Options in the White Paper on the Personal Tax and Transfer System: A General Equilibrium Approach* (Quebec: Université Laval, Département d'économique, 1984), Table A, p. xi.

benefits are also subject to confiscatory tax rates when they return to work. Hence, the efficiency gains from a marginal tax rate of less than 100 percent are likely to be very large for UI as well. Surely this is what UI ought to be: a fall-back system that encourages the recently un-employed to return to work, rather than, as it is now, a source of support that can be viewed as a payment for not working. It is for this reason that in Chapter 7 I argued for a slight reduction in benefits — to 50 percent of insurable earnings from 60 percent — combined with a reduction in the marginal tax rate on income earned while on UI benefits to 50 percent from 100 percent.

This discussion of the Quebec White Paper may appear to be excessively detailed, particularly given that the present study is directed largely toward social policy reform at the federal level. In fact, the White Paper is highly relevant here, since the underlying issues that it addresses are precisely the trilogy of challenges — fiscal, economic, and sociodemographic — that underpin this analysis. Moreover, although it is unlikely that much of the White Paper will appear immediately as legislation, it is likely that some of its proposals will be implemented. Other provinces will be motivated by their own concerns — and perhaps by the Quebec White Paper as well — to undertake comparable assessments of their systems. Such an assessment is already under way in Ontario. These provincial developments relate to yet another theme of the present study, namely, the critical role of provincial innovation and experimentation — that is, federation economics — in the evolution of social policy. Since most of the provincial initiatives are or will be in the direction of work-incentive-oriented income guarantees or of negative income tax systems, they are certain to provide valuable insights into integration methods, instrument design, delivery technology, and the economic effects of GAI mechanisms.

## The Financing of CAP

For many years, the poorer provinces have campaigned to alter the funding formula for the Canada Assistance Plan. In large measure, the argument for change is based on the incidence-of-welfare figures that appear in column 2 of Table 14. Although it is not always the provinces with a high incidence of welfare that spend more than the national per capita average on welfare, the affected provinces no doubt would reply that their overall fiscal positions constrain their ability to spend more than they do at present.

Given the overall fiscal challenge at the federal level, it would seem to be very unlikely that the provinces will be able to convince Ottawa to sweeten the CAP program. However, there are some factors that operate to strengthen the provinces' case. The first of these is the welfare "fallout'', created by the volatility of regional fortunes. For example, the recent dramatic economic downturn in Alberta has added considerably to the welfare rolls in some Atlantic provinces, since many laid-off workers have returned home and exhausted their UI benefits. The likelihood that the province of employment will not be the province of income support or welfare is likely to increase in an environment that calls for restructuring and adjustment. Since adjustment can and ought to be viewed as a national objective, it is not unreasonable for Ottawa to assume more of the burden for workers who are caught up in the downside of the adjustment process, regardless of their residence. The second factor is more important. To the extent that revisions in UI lead to an increased reliance on provincial welfare systems, Ottawa has a responsibility to carry some of this financial burden.

One proposal that has been floated recently is that the federal CAP payments be "equalized". For example, Ottawa would continue to limit its overall contribution to the funding of CAP to 50 percent — and thereby acknowledge the fiscal imperative — but its transfer to each province would either exceed 50 percent or fall short of it, depending on whether the province's incidence of welfare recipients was higher or lower than the average incidence (column 2, Table 14).

While I recognize the underlying concern, I do not believe that expenditure equalization is the solution. No other federation has a revenue-sharing program that is as comprehensive and as generous as Canada's. To begin the equalization process anew on the expenditure side would be to undermine the existing equalization system. Under that system, equalization payments are unconditional transfers — the provinces can use the money as they please. Expenditure-side equalization, by definition, would involve conditional payments and, therefore, a loss of provincial autonomy. Moreover, the process would tend to become open-ended: should Ontario not receive greater postsecondary grants per capita than, say, Prince Edward Island, since the latter province has neither Ontario's large number of expensive postgraduate institutions nor its burden of having to pay North American salaries to maintain world-class faculties?

A far better approach is available: for the federal government to make use of refundable tax credits, either within the personal income tax system or within the proposed value-added tax or business transfer tax. This approach is outlined in the following chapter, which deals with the family benefits tax transfer system. For present purposes, it is enough to note that a greater reliance on refundable tax credits would imply an enhanced role for the federal government in the area of basic income support. Under the assumption that welfare levels in Toronto need to be substantially higher than those in rural New Brunswick or even in towns such as Moncton and Kenora, an enlarged system of federal refundable tax credits would automatically provide a greater percentage of welfare costs in the latter areas. In this important sense, initiatives of this kind also can be viewed as an implicit "equalization" system for the provinces or regions with a high incidence of welfare obligations. As an added benefit, such initiatives would provide an incentive for those on welfare to reenter the labor force, since the benefits would be income-tested; that is, the marginal tax rate or the tax credits would be much less than 100 percent.

## Further Issues

The fact that responsibility for the welfare system is shared both among the provinces and between the provinces and the federal government raises a number of issues in addition to those related to work incentives and funding. None of these issues is in itself large enough to trigger any major reforms of the system. In combination, however, they merit attention in any redesign of the social policy network. The menu of concerns that follows is meant to be illustrative rather than exhaustive.

One broad issue is the substantial variation across provinces in the conditions of eligibility for welfare. An important aspect of this issue, as Kesselman points out, is the problem of the "harrassing provisions currently applied to unemployed employable applicants" in many jurisdictions; these provisions "are particularly difficult for younger and single persons in many provinces."[7] The provinces are, of course, within their rights when it comes to setting benefit levels and applying eligibility standards. Nevertheless, it should still be possible to move in the direction of harmonizing the system so that if an applicant were eligible for welfare in province A, he or she also would be eligible in province B. The federal government already attaches some conditions to its 50 percent funding, such as a requirement that the residency period for eligibility be minimal. The time has probably come, however, for Ottawa — or preferably the provinces themselves — to eliminate at least some of the arbitrariness that appears to be associated with qualifying for welfare. The equality provisions of the Charter of Rights and Freedoms are likely to have a major impact here, particularly in limiting the ability of provincial welfare systems to discriminate on the basis of age or marital status.

These federal-provincial concerns go both ways, however. Consider, for example, the operations of the Canada Employment Centres (CECs). No doubt they are closely integrated with the operations of the UI program, since both programs come under the same federal ministry. Not only are UI claimants required to register with the CECs, but the so-called

---

[7]Jonathan R. Kesselman, "Comparative Income Security for Canadians," in Vaillancourt, ed., *Income Distribution and Economic Security in Canada,* p. 305.

developmental uses of UI (work-sharing, job creation, and skill-training activities) presumably are directed principally at UI claimants. Given this structure, there may well be a tendency for the CECs to overlook welfare claimants who are able to work — and who are probably more in need of training and job creation programs than are UI claimants. This possibility represents a concern worthy of attention. Certainly it is of concern to the provinces. Under the proposed UI reform, which would transfer employment-creating activities out of UI, this problem might be alleviated.

Reform of the welfare work subsystem could pave the way for some novel initiatives in the area of job creation. First of all, a rationalization of UI would free up a substantial sum of money, some of which would presumably find its way into job creation programs. Second, job creation programs would become more effective if the tax rates in the transition from unemployment to work were reduced. Third, the persistence of high unemployment appears to be increasing the willingness of policymakers, both federal and provincial, to become more innovative with respect to employment enhancement. For example, the Quebec White Paper proposes higher support levels for welfare recipients who are willing to undergo retraining. Moreover, there is now serious consideration of wage subsidies, whether to employers or employees, as an alternative to traditional forms of job creation. Although one should be leery of calls for the wholesale adoption of new job creation strategies, greater flexibility and innovation in program design clearly are warranted.

Not surprisingly, the persistence of high unemployment rates — and of forecasts that progress in reducing these rates likely will be slow — has produced a remarkable growth of community-based approaches to the unemployment problem. Many of these approaches use welfare or UI as the basic support system. Some also make extensive use of the underground economy or nonmarket exchange systems. Coinciding with this development is an increased interest in community-based development in academic circles and in some provincial governments.

It is appropriate to question whether the centralized system of Canada Employment Centres and centrally directed job creation programs are able to accommodate this emerging diversity. Moreover, since it is difficult to argue that the regional development programs have been successful over the years, it seems only prudent to encourage these grassroots initiatives, at least until it becomes possible to measure their success. Indeed, it may well be appropriate to introduce more flexibility into the operations of CECs, even to the point of experimenting on a meaningful scale with subcontracting their activities to private-sector agencies on a performance evaluation basis. These observations are consistent with the view which I endorsed earlier, that the ongoing evolution on the economic front is likely to call for greater decentralization than has prevailed heretofore.

In short, there appears to be plenty of room for positive-sum negotiation between Ottawa and the provinces with respect to the operations of the welfare system and the manner in which it interacts with other programs in the welfare work subsystem.

Two further concerns merit discussion. One arises from the fact that it is possible, under existing arrangements, for one level of government to transfer the responsibility for income support to the other. The Nova Scotia job corps programs of the mid-1970s, for example, provided 12 weeks of employment at the minimum wage for the unemployed — the exact number of weeks required in 1978 to qualify individuals for UI for the remainder of the year. In terms of any benefit-cost calculation, a program of this kind makes eminent sense for a province, particularly if the individuals employed are removed from the provincial welfare rolls. It hardly qualifies, however, as an appropriate policy from the point of view of the participants or of the economy as a whole.

Incentives for buck-passing will always exist in a decentralized federation. At best, the incentives can be limited. Indeed, the proposals in Chapter 7, which would return UI to insurance principles and eliminate arrangements that overly reward short-term employment in high unemployment regions, would minimize the degree to which the provinces find such initiatives appealing. Moreover, the proposals that are detailed in Chapter 9, dealing with the family benefits package of the income tax system, would do much to cushion the impact on provincial welfare systems of a rationalization of the UI system.

The second concern has to do with provincial minimum wage policy. It is anomalous, to say the least, that the pattern of minimum wages across provinces often bears little resemblance to average provincial wages. For example, there have been periods in which Ontario has had one of the lowest, if not the lowest, minimum wage levels, while Quebec until recently had the highest minimum wage, not only in Canada but in North America. Situations of this kind arise, in part, because provinces can transfer the costs of an anomalous minimum wage policy to the rest of the country, through the federal government. Consider the impact of an increase in the minimum wage rate that leads to an increase in unemployment. Ottawa comes to the rescue with UI transfers, one-half of any welfare costs, and increased equalization (for have-not provinces). This series of offsets substantially lessens the economic costs of having a minimum wage at a level that results in reduced employment.

The real point here is not that the provinces should be required to set their minimum wages at an appropriate level. Rather, it is that the interactions in the welfare work subsystem should not be such that they exempt the provinces from bearing the lion's share of the economic costs of their own policies. The complexity of design and purpose that characterizes the welfare work subsystem makes it virtually impossible to eliminate all of these negative externalities. Nonetheless, as was noted above, they can be minimized. Indeed, one argument against initiating an equalization component for CAP expenditures is that this step would add to the externalities: if Ottawa were responsible for, say, 75 percent of welfare expenditures in provinces with a high incidence of welfare claims, the cost to these provinces of maintaining inappropriate levels for their minimum wages would be correspondingly reduced.

## *Summary*

The agenda for reforming the CAP has basically to do with addressing the economic and sociodemographic challenges, although failure to address them will mean that the system also will encounter the fiscal challenge. Currently, the federal government's portion of welfare spending amounts to just over $4 billion. However, the Nielsen Task Force estimated that if the number of employables receiving welfare continues to increase, the federal cost could be $8.45 billion by fiscal year 1989–90.[8]

Chapter 11 discusses the specific proposals for reforming the CAP and the manner in which these proposals relate to the welfare work subsystem.

---

[8]Canada, Task Force on Program Review, *Canada Assistance Plan*, a Study Team Report to the Task Force (Ottawa: Supply and Services Canada, 1985), p. 5.

# 9

## *The Family Benefits Package*

### *The Status Quo*

Information on the range and costs of family benefits appears in Table 2 (in Chapter 3). For convenience, Table 17 reproduces these figures, with the addition of some estimates of the fiscal impact of the benefits on provincial governments. Family allowances cost the federal government just under $2 billion in 1984, but because they are taxable they *added* $225 million to provincial income tax revenues. Because the child tax credit is a federal responsibility, it has no direct impact on provincial finances. The exemptions do, however: the costs to the provinces of the child tax exemption and spousal exemption were $430 million and $693 million respectively in 1984. Overall, then, the family benefits package cost the federal government about $5.48 billion and the provincial governments $898 million.

It is essential to recognize these federal-provincial linkages in the delivery of family benefits when contemplating reform of the system. For example, as a result of the 1985 federal budget, family allowance benefits will be indexed annually to the extent that the Consumer Price Index increases by more than 3 percentage points. The child tax credit will be increased in steps from its 1985 level of $384 to $524 in 1988, when it too will be indexed (as above). The child tax exemption, currently $710, will be reduced gradually until 1989, when it will equal the level of family allowances; thereafter, it will move in tandem with family allowances. In passing, it should be noted that this latter provision, which sets the child tax exemption equal to the level of family allowances, is effectively equivalent to the combination of a) eliminating the child tax exemption entirely and b) making family allowances nontaxable. Both approaches ensure that, other things being equal, families with children receive additional after-tax income. This recognizes the long-standing horizontal equity aspect of the Canadian personal income tax system, namely that the PIT system takes account of children in determining net taxes payable.

Together, these measures imply that in 1988 family benefits will be targeted to a much greater degree than they are now. Moreover, the implications of these changes for provincial personal income tax revenues are quite significant. Since the child tax credit is a federal program, the substantial increase in the level of the credit will not affect provincial finances.

### Table 17
### Expenditures on Family Benefits, 1984
*($ millions)*

| Benefit | Federal government | | | Provincial governments[a] |
| | Expenditure | Tax revenue cost | Total | |
|---|---|---|---|---|
| Family allowances | 2,360 | −450 | 1,910 | −225 |
| Child tax exemption | — | 860 | 860 | 430 |
| Child tax credit | — | 1,325 | 1,325 | 0 |
| Total child benefits | 2,360 | 1,735 | 4,095 | 205 |
| Spousal exemption (1986–87) [b] | — | 1,385 | — | 693 |
| *Total* | *2,360* | *3,120* | *5,480* | *898* |

[a]Estimated, on the assumption that the provinces collect one-third of all personal income taxes.
[b]From Table 2.
Source: Canada, Minister of National Health and Welfare, *Child and Elderly Benefits* (Ottawa, January 1985), p.25.

But the provinces will *gain* revenue from both the increase in family allowances and the reduction in the level of the child tax exemption. Indeed, it was this anticipated increase in provincial income tax revenues that, in part at least, led the federal government recently to pare down the growth of provincial transfers associated with the established programs.

The federal-provincial interaction has other interesting implications. For example, if Ottawa increased family allowances or the child tax credit, the family benefits package might very well become substantially more "progressive" in its distribution of income. It does not follow, however, that the *system* also could become more progressive. Were the provinces to respond by freezing their overall welfare benefit levels (which include these family benefits), they would, in effect, simply transfer the increase from the federal government to their own treasuries. Indeed, the reform proposals contained in the Quebec White Paper do exactly this: increases in federal family allowances would make no difference to the overall support package for welfare recipients and the working poor, since they would be fully offset within the Quebec guarantee level. This consideration clearly places a premium on federal-provincial cooperation and coordination as far as reform of this component of the subsystem is concerned.

This interaction has implications for another aspect of social policy reform — the issue of the universality of individual programs. As I argued in the introductory analytical chapters, the fact that one component program of a subsystem is universal may be quite irrelevant to the operation of the system as a whole. The Quebec example is highly relevant here, since the White Paper proposals effectively would convert the universal federal family allowance payments into targeted or income-tested benefits for Quebec recipients. In the final analysis, it is the characteristics of the overall system that matter, not the characteristics of an individual program within the system.

## Pressures and Opportunities for Reform

### The Fiscal Challenge

One of the motivating forces underlying the social policy review is the fiscal challenge. Indeed, in calling for the review, Finance Minister Wilson stated that Canada "must direct more resources to those most in need...and reduce the after-tax value of benefits going to higher-income Canadians."[1] Thus, one implication of viewing reform from the perspective of the fiscal challenge is that not all of the resulting savings would be redeployed within the family benefits system. Some would go toward reducing the deficit or, more likely, toward reducing marginal tax rates. There is a certain equity in this approach, since the savings would be obtained from depriving the middle- and upper-income classes of benefits and/or deductions. Hence, it would be appropriate to pass some of these savings back in the form of a general reduction in marginal tax rates, particularly since the United States is now well on its way toward a dramatic lowering of its marginal tax rates.

In any event, the family benefits package lends itself well to meeting the needs of the fiscal challenge; even with an enrichment of programs for those most in need, a move toward greater selectivity or better targeting of benefits can generate considerable savings. This was, of course, the thrust of the recommendations in Chapter 6 relating to the retirement income subsystem.

### Increasing the Emphasis on Refundable Tax Credits

The major result of the seemingly abortive social policy review process in the 1970s was the introduction in 1978 of the refundable child tax credit. Family allowances were rolled back dramatically and replaced by the refundable child tax credit. Not only did this measure more effectively target funds for children to those families most in need — that is, it was a move away from universality — but in the process, the total number of dollars devoted to child benefits tripled. Of equal importance, however, was the fact that the introduction of the refundable tax credit

---

[1]Michael H. Wilson, *Securing Economic Renewal: The Budget Speech, delivered in the House of Commons, February 26, 1986* (Ottawa: Department of Finance, 1986), p. 12.

represented a significant, albeit incremental, move in the direction of a GAI or an NIT. The current round of family benefits proposals will enhance even further the role of refundable child tax credits within the overall family benefits package, although this time the increase in refundable child tax credits will be, as noted above, at the expense of the child tax exemption.

This process can go only so far, however, toward instituting a GAI or toward meeting the concerns, discussed in Chapter 8, that arise from the possibility of spillovers from UI reform to provincial welfare schemes. At some point, the personal income tax has to make the philosophical and political leap to extend the refundable tax credit concept to adults. In principle, the obvious route to follow is to convert the personal and spousal exemptions into refundable credits. In practice, however, this may be a difficult step, since the personal income tax system already carries an enormous load in the system. It is the principal source of government revenues. Through the RRSP provisions, it is a means of encouraging retirement savings, and in this context it is actually a tax on expenditures rather than on income. It is also used to favor some types of income (for example, capital gains) relative to others. And so on. To use the income tax system as the principal delivery mechanism for a GAI would amount to foregoing its use for these other important goals, or at least to subordinate them to the larger concerns of a GAI. Not surprisingly, governments are not keen on having their fiscal hands tied in this manner, as the review process in the 1970s made abundantly clear.

The mid-1980s environment, however, differs in one crucial respect from that of the mid-1970s. Enter the business transfer tax and PIT reform.

### The Business Transfer Tax

Intriguingly, if Ottawa moves ahead with its proposed value-added tax, the so-called business transfer tax, this step will open up a whole new range of possibilities for the family benefits component of the welfare work subsystem. For one thing, a BTT is a very effective revenue generator. Therefore, introduction of the proposed BTT would take considerable pressure off the PIT, making it possible to reduce marginal tax rates substantially. Such a reduction by itself would serve to target more effectively a whole range of social policy benefits. For example, the value of all tax deductions, whether for spouses, RRSPs, or the elderly, would decrease with a decrease in marginal tax rates. With lower marginal tax rates, it would also be easier to implement tax-back schemes on benefits such as welfare and UI, since the "aggregate" tax-back rate would now be less likely to become confiscatory.

The greater degree of freedom that the PIT system would obtain in the presence of a BTT would facilitate the system's eventual use as the vehicle for a GAI. There is also, however, a more direct and important way in which the introduction of a BTT would promote the development of a GAI. Since the BTT would be far less progressive than a tax on income, it is likely that the federal government would incorporate some sort of refundable tax credit as part of the BTT in order to increase its progressivity. A BTT tax credit presumably would be run through the income tax system and, in effect, would become yet another component of the overall support system for low-income Canadians. But one with a major difference: in effect, the BTT credit would be a refundable tax credit for *adults* or families. Combined with the already proposed changes in the refundable child tax credit, this arrangement would accomplish not only a very substantial degree of benefit targeting but also a quite dramatic move along the way to a GAI. Actually, the family benefits package has already moved in this direction. For the 1986 taxation year, the federal government introduced a refundable sales tax credit for families. The refundable BTT credit for low-income Canadians would provide a substantial enrichment of this new tax credit.

## PIT Reform

With the savings that would arise from greater targeting of benefits in both the retirement income and welfare work subsystems and with the advent of a BTT, the stage would be set for substantial PIT reform. Indeed, the purposes of a special BTT tax credit for low-income families could be accomplished instead by a redesign of the PIT system. For example, the spousal and personal benefits could be converted into refundable tax credits, which, while desirable in their own right, would also lessen the regressivity of the BTT for low-income family units. Just how far one proceeds along this path — for example, one might increase the personal and spousal exemptions in the process of converting them into refundable credits — is not as important as taking the initial critical steps. This observation is in line with the earlier suggestion that neither the delivery technology nor our information about economic impacts is sufficiently advanced to permit the implementation of a GAI in one step. But the timing and the environment *are* propitious for embarking on a set of initiatives that will facilitate a natural evolution toward a full-blown GAI if Canadians deem such a course to be viable and desirable.

## Conclusion

It is important at this juncture to recognize the underlying thrust of the reforms pertaining to the welfare work subsystem proposed in this and the two preceding chapters. In one sense, the outcome of the reforms would be quite dramatic — the advent of a BTT, base broadening and

lower marginal tax rates for the PIT, a return of UI to insurance principles, and a conversion of the family benefits components of the PIT to
refundable credits — thereby paving the way for an eventual incentive-
oriented GAI — and so on. In another sense, however, the overall reform
process would not be as dramatic as it might appear to be at first glance.
No program would be eliminated, and many of the proposed changes
reflect shifts in philosophy as much as they do shifts in impact. To put
the matter somewhat differently, the proposed process of change can be
viewed as one of measured incrementalism across a wide spectrum of
programs. Moreover, most, if not all, of the proposed innovations are not
only consistent with the trilogy of challenges underpinning this study
but have received substantial support from the growing body of socio-
economic literature.

One could argue that what has been lacking is the political will to embark on such a reform. Although there may be something to this argument, I think that some more fundamental principle has been at work.
From a political point of view, public policy in modern societies is inherently so complex and individual policies are so closely intertwined
that it is extremely difficult to single out one policy area for major reform. Given the political necessity of compensating the losers from major
reform of any single program, the end result is likely to be as problemat-
ic as the status quo. In the current environment, however, the fiscal, sociodemographic, and economic challenges on the social policy front have
been joined by the external pressure of tax reform in the United States,
to create a unique "window of opportunity" to engage in reform across
a wide range of policy fronts. What this window of opportunity offers
is the unusual luxury of providing the requisite compensation for losers
that arise from changes in one program through appropriate alterations
in other programs. In other words, there are sufficient degrees of policy
freedom in play both to accomplish the desired reform objectives and
to put in place initiatives that are both consistent with this reform and
adequate in terms of compensating those Canadians who may feel short-
changed by one aspect or another of the reform.

One example will suffice. The previous chapter raised the concern that
the elimination of regional benefits could result in greater fiscal pressure
on the provinces, since many UI exhaustees probably would fall back on
the welfare system for support. However, adoption of the proposals for
enhanced refundable child tax credits and a BTT refundable tax credit —
or the more thorough reform of converting spousal and personal PIT exemptions into refundable credits — would provide a federally funded,
minimum support level for all low-income Canadians on which the
provincial welfare programs could build. Because this minimum federal
level would be income tested, the provinces henceforth would find it

much easier to design welfare systems that provided substantial incentive for the transition from welfare to work. Moreover, if one assumes that welfare support levels bear some relation to the average income in the province, the establishment of a uniform federal minimum level across the country would have its greatest value precisely for those provinces that might suffer fiscally from any UI reform. In other words, the ability to embark on meaningful reform is substantially enhanced in an environment where both the generation of benefits and incentives and the compensation of losers can be integrated into system reform rather than undertaken in the context of the reform of a single program.

With these comments as backdrop, the stage is now set for drawing together the proposed package of reforms for the welfare work subsystem. No analysis of this general area would be complete, however, without a description and evaluation of the very comprehensive reform package proposed by the Macdonald Commission and also the UI reforms contained in the Forget Report. This is the purpose of the next chapter.

# 10

# The Proposals of the Macdonald and Forget Commissions

## The Macdonald Commission's Proposals: A Description

Given the very broad mandate of the Royal Commission on the Economic Union and Development Prospects for Canada (Macdonald Commission), it is hardly surprising that among its many recommendations was a series of proposals to redesign the welfare work subsystem. Without going into excessive detail, one can address the Macdonald Commission's approach to reform by focusing on its three key sets of recommendations in this area.

### Unemployment Insurance

The first set of recommendations relates to unemployment insurance. Basically, the Macdonald Commission recommended that the UI program revert to insurance principles. Among its specific recommendations for UI, the Commission suggested:

- reducing the benefit rate to 50 percent of earnings;
- raising the entrance requirements to 15 to 20 weeks of insured work over the preceding year;
- tightening the link between the maximum benefit period and the minimum employment period: for example, establish a ratio of two or three weeks of work to qualify for one week of benefits; and
- eliminating the regional differentiation within the unemployment insurance program.[1]

In addition, the Commission recommended that premium rates be related more closely to the risk of layoff. It rationalized these proposals as follows:

> To eliminate the regional differentiation of the UI program would encourage rather than discourage — as does the present system —

---

[1]Canada, Royal Commission on the Economic Union and Development Prospects for Canada (Macdonald Commission), *Report*, vol. 2 (Ottawa: Supply and Services Canada, 1985), p. 611.

labour movement towards regions with higher levels of employment. The existing system tends to perpetuate regional unemployment differentials, and this situation, together with the absence of experience rating, tends to reinforce the concentration of temporary and unstable jobs in high-unemployment and low-wage regions.

The other suggested changes to the benefits structure are meant to encourage steadier job attachments, more intensive job search during periods of unemployment, and a higher proportion of job search while employed....

The proposed changes to the benefit structure also reflect this Commission's view that the UI program has become too large relative to other labour-market programs, and that the employment opportunities for Canadians would be improved by switching some funds from UI support to programs organized to facilitate adjustment to technological and economic change.[2]

## *The Transitional Adjustment Assistance Plan*

Some of the savings resulting from the Macdonald Commission's redesign of UI would be reflected in lower UI premiums. Most, however, would be allocated to the Commission's second major recommendation for the welfare work subsystem, the creation of a "Transitional Adjustment Assistance Plan" (TAAP). This would be an omnibus program designed to allow the Canadian labor force to adjust to emerging employment opportunities. It would provide funding for on-the-job training programs, wage subsidy programs, early retirement plans, mobility grants, and special projects. Since part of the funds for a TAAP would derive from the elimination of regional extended benefits, one would expect that there would be a regional component to such a program. As far as eligibility is concerned, a TAAP would direct considerable effort to prime-age and older workers with a labor force attachment of at least five years. In this respect, it would be a type of unemployment insurance program for long-term workers who become unemployed.

In commenting on the combination of the UI reforms and the proposal for introducing a TAAP, the Commission states that the proposals "would replace the anti-adjustment features of unemployment insurance with the positive adjustment feature of TAAP, [an arrangement that would] serve greatly to enhance labour-force flexibility and adaptability."[3]

## *The Universal Income Security Program*

The third component of the Macdonald Commission's package was a guaranteed annual income scheme — the "Universal Income Security Pro-

---

[2]Ibid., pp. 611–612.
[3]Ibid., p. 619.

gram'' (UISP). The most comprehensive version of UISP would replace these existing social programs:

- the GIS (but not the OAS);
- family allowances;
- child tax credits;
- personal exemptions;
- married exemptions;
- federal contributions to social assistance (for example, CAP); and
- federal social housing policies.

In place of all of these programs, Ottawa would transfer roughly $9,000 to a family of four. This would be taxed back at a 20 percent rate, for a break-even point in the neighborhood of $45,000 — that is, at $45,000 of earned income, a 20 percent tax rate would generate $9,000 in taxes and completely offset the initial guarantee. Actually, the break-even income level under UISP would be lower than this, since the 20 percent tax-back rate for UISP would be in addition to the taxes that would arise from the operation of the regular income tax system. Moreover, income taxes would begin to apply rather quickly, since under this version of UISP all personal exemptions would be removed.[4]

The provinces, for their part, would have two polar choices open to them — to use the monies currently directed toward the CAP to top up the federal program or to cede some personal income tax points to Ottawa and, in effect, vacate the income support field; presumably, they would also be able to adopt positions that lie between these extremes.

Although this brief review of the Macdonald Commission's proposals for reform of the welfare work subsystem has of necessity left out many details, it is sufficiently complete to permit an evaluation of these proposals.

### *The Macdonald Commission's Proposals: An Evaluation*

The Commission's proposals for reforming UI and introducing a TAAP are, in general, consistent with the analysis in Chapter 7. This is hardly surprising, since parts of that analysis were based on the Commission's work. Although the specific proposals for UI reform in the following chapter will differ somewhat from those of the Commission, I would have

---

[4]An alternative version of UISP would maintain the personal exemptions under the income tax system and be offset by a smaller overall guarantee. Otherwise, the scheme would be the same.

little trouble in accepting the Commission's views as a fallback position. The goals are clearly similar — to modify UI in the context of the welfare work subsystem in ways that would create an incentive to work, encourage adjustment, and foster employment creation.

The Commission estimates that its proposals for UI likely would reduce the costs of UI "by not less than 35 to 40 percent or about $4 billion at 1985 levels of unemployment."[5] Some recent empirical work by Suzanne Lévesque of Laval University has provided further evidence relating to the likely impact of the Commission's proposals. Lévesque's analysis indicates that the implementation of these proposals would reduce the *number* of UI claimants in Quebec by 21 percent for adult females, by 13 percent for adult males, and by 34 percent for the young (under 25 years, both sexes). The corresponding results for Ontario are 15, 12, and 28 percent, and for Saskatchewan they are 13, 15, and 23 percent.[6] The results suggest, in general, that these proposals would have their greatest impact on the young and on adult women. This outcome is consistent with the fact that it is these groups that would be most affected by the tightening up of UI and the increased emphasis on insurance principles. On the other hand, it is precisely these groups, particularly the young, that ought to be helped by the job creation components of a program such as a TAAP.

While I obviously support the concept of a TAAP-type program to promote job creation and labor force adjustment, some aspects of the Macdonald Commission's TAAP proposal appear wanting. As Kesselman has noted:

> Under the suggested eligibility criteria, the Commission noted that concentrating the $4 billion of annual TAAP funds on the 253,000 workers who in 1984 had been unemployed at least one year would yield benefits of $15,801 per worker, and that further restricting the program to 150,000 would raise the per capita benefits to $26,700. The Commission also proposed that TAAP benefits for individual participants be proportional to the length of time in the labour force up to a maximum of 15 or 20 years.[7]

Kesselman expresses considerable concern about the operations of a TAAP, noting that the program's administrators would have "considerable

[5] Macdonald Commission, *Report*, vol. 2., p. 613.

[6] Suzanne Lévesque, "Déterminants du taux de participation à l'Assurance-chômage et programmes d'aide sociale" (Ph.D. diss., Université Laval, Département d'économique, 1986), Tables 14, 15, and 16.

[7] Jonathan R. Kesselman, "The Royal Commission's Proposals for Income Security Reform," *Canadian Public Policy* 12 (February 1986): 104.

discretion over the choice of beneficiaries with resultant potential for major inequities."[8]

My concerns with a TAAP are more fundamental. As proposed, it is really still a part of UI, focusing on long-term workers. Although this group of beneficiaries is obviously meritorious, the employment and skill-enhancing role of a major program such as a TAAP ought to be directed to *all* Canadians who are willing to undertake activities or training designed to enhance their work prospects. In other words, such a program should operate *outside* the parameters of UI.

In the following chapter, I shall recommend that some provision for long-term service be incorporated in UI, but that any job creation and economic adjustment program be designed and operated independently of UI.

My evaluation of the Commission's UISP proposal is considerably less favorable. Although the proposal does address some of the concerns I have raised about the operation of the welfare system and the family benefits package, it does so in a way that runs afoul of the fiscal challenge. My concern over the prospective costs of UISP has several aspects. First, although under current arrangements the tax rate associated with the transition from welfare to work is probably over 100 percent, lowering it to 20 percent is inappropriate. This tax-back rate is far too low, since it would place family units that earn in the neighborhood of $30,000 to $40,000 in a much more favorable position with regard to the tax system than they are at present. Although it is clearly desirable to provide some income supplementation for the working poor, this support should not be operative at levels of income as high as $30,000 to $40,000. Second, note that the average taxpayer would lose not only the tax exemption for his or her spouse but also his or her own exemption. These provisions represent a very substantial tax hike at a time when personal income tax rates are already much higher than those in the United States. Third, the proposal is remarkably insensitive to some of the political realities. The abolition of family allowances and personal exemptions would be more of a revolutionary change than an evolutionary one. It is possible to move toward a guaranteed annual income while maintaining most of the politically sensitive features of the present income tax system. Finally, the UISP proposal appears to come out of the blue. There is no background support for this program, let alone an evaluation of its likely impact, in the 70 research monographs produced for the Macdonald Commission.

For all of these reasons, the UISP approach appears to be unacceptable. However, should Canadians desire to take a big bang approach, rather

---

[8]Ibid.

than an incremental approach, to income support, there is a way to make a UISP-type program more acceptable. Basically, this approach would involve the use of a tax-back rate of 50 percent rather than the proposed 20 percent rate. This arrangement would still allow the scheme to accomplish its integration and incentive goals while averting its collision course with the fiscal challenge.

Nonetheless, the present study takes the view that the preferable approach on the income support front is an evolutionary or incremental one. In this context, the concept of a GAI or a UISP is important principally as a longer-term benchmark toward which the system might eventually evolve. Therefore, as I said earlier, it makes sense to ensure that reform proposals are consistent with the eventual adaption of a GAI, even though a full-blown GAI or UISP is not appropriate at present.

## The Forget Commission

The Commission of Inquiry on Unemployment Insurance (Forget Commission) tabled its *Report* in mid-November 1986.[9] Because the manuscript of the present study was essentially in final form by then, the analysis and recommendations of the Commission are not well integrated into the various chapters of my own analysis.

The Forget Commission's *Report* is actually several reports: in addition to the main report, the document contained four supplementary statements by commissioners, including one of nearly 100 pages by F.J. Soboda and J.J. Munro. Most of the brief description and evaluation that follows, however, will focus on the main report.

For purposes of presentation it is useful to attempt to separate the Commission's assessment of the unemployment problems in Canada from its recommendations for a new UI program.

### The Plight of the Unemployed

Contrary to what one might have been led to believe from the newspaper headlines prior to its publication, the *Report* is a very compassionate document, at least in terms of its assessment of the problems faced by Canada's unemployed. In the margins of its pages, for example, are over 400 excerpts from the Commission's hearings. These are the voices of individual Canadians speaking to the trials, tribulations, and even despair of a life of unemployment, to the impenetrable red tape associated with the UI program, to their helplessness before the administrators of UI, and to their sense of unfairness associated with the combination of mid-career skill obsolescence and the preferences of

---

[9]Canada, Commission of Inquiry on Unemployment Insurance (Forget Commission), *Report* (Ottawa: Supply and Services Canada, 1986).

employers for younger workers. Also included are concerns about the incentives of the UI program: regionally extended benefits come under attack and so does the January 1, 1986, decision to treat pension income as earnings for UI purposes. While the vast majority of these comments are limited to a paragraph, at least a dozen are several pages in length. Taken together, they constitute in effect, a report within a report. In my view, the Commission is to be congratulated for the way in which it has integrated this evidence from the cross-country hearings into its analysis. Perhaps this is a common occurrence in other disciplines, but it is surely rare in commission reports on economic issues.

Most of the analysis in the first half of the *Report* focuses on the needs of the unemployed — that is, on the series of policy measures that will enhance their opportunities for rejoining the work force. As a result, one major thrust of the *Report* is a focus on combating adult illiteracy and innumeracy and, more generally, on training and retraining. The *Report* also argues, however, that greater flexibility and innovation must filter into the traditional and too frequently centralized job creation programs. Community economic development initiatives merit attention as do flexibility in work arrangements and labor-force attachment. As part of this increased flexibility, the *Report* recommends a consolidation of the various existing federal programs designed to facilitate mobility into a single program characterized by greater access.

These and similar sections of the *Report* do not bear directly on UI. Rather, they are geared toward improving employment prospects for all Canadians. They do address UI indirectly, however, since the *Report* eventually argues that the monies currently allocated to the income support aspects of UI — such as regionally extended benefits — as distinct from the social insurance aspects, are better spent on programs for skill enhancement or job creation initiatives that will generate enhanced employment or reemployment prospects.

## The Role of UI in the Overall Income Support, Income Replacement System

The *Report* envisages, perhaps drawing from the Newfoundland Royal Commission, a three-tier system for income security: income support (for example, welfare), income supplementation (for example, the various provincial income supplementation programs for low-income workers), and social insurance (for example, UI, workers' compensation and the CPP/QPP). Actually, the analysis in this section is a bit confused. For example, the *Report* classifies OAS as an income supplementation program whereas GIS is put under the income support category. Surely, the reverse is the more appropriate classification. Nonetheless, the recommendations with respect to UI (to be detailed later) depend in no small measure on the assumption that Canada has in place a comprehensive program of both income support and income supplementation. In particular, the Commission recommends that Canada embark on an "earnings supplementation program". Recommendation 8 states:

> The Canadian government should work closely with the provinces to develop earnings supplementation programs that complement the proposed changes in the Unemployment Insurance program. These programs should ensure that those who participate in the labour force but have inadequate incomes would be eligible to receive a supplement on the basis of total household income rather than individual income. The tax-back rate, when combined with the income tax system, should be less than 50 percent.[10]

This is, of course, the big bang solution to income security — a universal, income-tested, work-oriented guaranteed annual income. In earlier chapters, I welcomed moves in this direction, such as the likely BTT low-income tax credit. I have also taken the position, however, that it is highly unlikely that Canada will move dramatically in this direction. To do so would require a monumental federal-provincial bargaining and consultation process. This does not seem possible in the immediate future. Nor would the imposition of a full-blown GAI appear appropriate at this juncture. Careful evaluation of intermediate steps such as the conversion of exemptions to credits, greater integration of the positive and negative sides of the tax system, and increased provincial experimentation with the incentive implications of alternative NIT instruments are absolutely critical in order that the tax transfer system is not saddled with an inappropriately costly and ineffective version of a GAI. It is noteworthy that the Forget Commission did not attempt to assign any dollar figure to this recommendation for an earnings supplementation scheme.

Nonetheless, the Commission's key recommendation for UI — the "annualization" proposal — is effectively predicated on the existence of a comprehensive earnings supplementation program.

## The Proposals for Reform

### Annualization

The Forget Commission's assessment of the shortcomings of the existing UI program differs from the assessment that appears in Chapter 7 and from that of the Macdonald Commission only in the way that the UI system should respond to these shortcomings. The Forget Commission

---

[10]Ibid., p. 119.

recommends that benefits be "annualized": each claimant would be entitled automatically to a full year of benefits — 50 weeks plus the two-week waiting period — and these benefits would be based on earnings over the full year prior to the claim. Specifically, the Commission suggests that:

- There would be a uniform entry requirement of 350 hours of work (roughly equivalent to 10 weeks) which would apply to all workers, including those applying for sickness and maternity benefits, as well as new entrants to the labour force, re-entrants and repeaters.
- Benefits after a transition period would be based upon average weekly earnings in the preceding 52 weeks and not, as now, on earnings in the preceding 10 to 20 weeks.
- Benefits would be paid in 50 weekly installments, after a two-week waiting period. This would eliminate the current practice of varying the duration of benefits according to weeks worked and regional rates of unemployment.
- During the course of the transition period, consideration would be given to increasing the level of benefits from the current 60 percent to 66 2/3 percent of insurable earnings.[11]

Thus, all benefit periods would be set uniformly at one year regardless of previous work experience, provided only that the minimum requirement of ten weeks was met. Note that these ten weeks need not be consecutive: ten weeks worked over the past year would satisfy the requirement. In one sense, this compulsory 52-week benefit period is not a major change from the status quo, since the current high unemployment rates — and, therefore, the triggering of regionally extended benefits — imply that most claimants now qualify for close to a year of benefits.

The major innovation occurs in the method of benefit payout. All claimants are eligible to receive in benefits two-thirds of their insurable earnings over the past year, but these must be paid out in equal installments over 50 weeks. Consider two individuals, both of whom earn $500 per week — essentially the maximum weekly insurable earnings level. Assume both file a UI claim, but one individual has worked for 50 weeks over the past year and the other for ten. The longer-term worker qualifies for two-thirds of his or her annual earnings of $25,000 (50 × $500) to be paid out over 50 weeks. Because that claimant also worked for 50 weeks, however, the benefit payment is equal to two-thirds of his or her insurable earnings — that is, $333.32. This would not differ much

[11]Ibid., p. 183.

from the current payout to a long-term worker except that, under the Forget Commission's proposal, the replacement rate would be increased from 60 percent to 66 2/3 percent.

The situation is quite different for the second claimant, who has worked for only ten weeks. The shorter-term worker's annual earnings are one-fifth of those of the longer-term worker, so the weekly benefit rate will also be one-fifth, or $66.67. Under the existing arrangements, the second claimant would qualify for a weekly benefit of $300 — that is, 60 percent of $500 — for a period that could be as long as 42 weeks if the regional unemployment rate exceeded 9 percent. In other words, the present system allows the worker to qualify for benefits of $12,600, based on earnings of $5,000. By contrast, annualization would ensure that maximum benefits will be two-thirds of insurable earnings for all claimants.

Note that by limiting the maximum payout to $3,333.33 — that is, two-thirds of the annual earnings of $5,000 — rather than $12,600 as under the current system, annualization indirectly eliminates regional benefits. The Forget Commission's proposals would use these savings to embark on the range of programs alluded to earlier — combating adult illiteracy and innumeracy, retraining, community development projects, and so on — in order to enhance the employability of economically disadvantaged Canadians.

It appears clear that annualization would have a major impact on those workers who use the present system as a means of adopting what is, for them, a preferred life-style. The prospect of giving up a $500 per week job after ten weeks to collect $66.67 per week on UI is not very appealing. Hence, for this class of worker, annualization presumably will induce longer labor force attachment.

For those workers who lose their jobs after temporary periods in the labor force, however, the annualization implications appear rather bleak. But it is precisely here that the underlying assumption of the existence of a comprehensive income support and income supplementation system comes into play. Households in need would have to resort to these underlying support mechanisms. UI is not supposed to serve this role: it is an insurance scheme that should provide replacement of earnings in the case of job loss or interruption of employment earnings, and the concept of annualization assumes that the settlement period is to be an annual rather than a weekly one.

This is my interpretation of the Forget Commission's annualization proposal. I shall attempt a more detailed evaluation after focusing on some of the Commission's other proposals relating to UI reform.

Other Reform Measures

The Forget Commission recommends that if individuals resort to work while on claim, earnings from work should be taxed at 66 2/3 percent against UI benefits. The underlying principle is that if a claimant with long-term labor force attachment prior to filing a claim rejoins the labor force at his or her previous salary, UI benefits will automatically fall to zero. By itself, this is clearly desirable, particularly compared with the current 100 percent tax on earnings beyond 25 percent of benefits. This proposal appears, however, to overlook the fact that in an earlier recommendation, the Commission argued for an earnings supplementation scheme (reproduced above) whereby market earnings, including UI, would decrease the income support level by 50 cents on the dollar. Taken together, this would imply confiscatory rates of tax on earnings while on UI. Hence, the Commission paid insufficient attention to the manner in which UI would mesh with the rest of the income security system.

Like the Macdonald Commission, and like the recommendations I proposed in Chapter 7, the Forget Commission proposes a "cumulative employment account" for workers with long-term (at least 30 years) labor force attachment, the funds being drawn for "reemployment" purposes such as retraining, education, or mobility.

Finally, the Commission has a host of recommendations relating to the detailed operations of the system (treatment of illness, maternity, severance pay, lockouts, and the like), to the organization of UI (organizational form, composition of board of directors, powers, regional structure), and to the accountability and control of UI. While these recommendations are no doubt very important, they are also somewhat beyond the narrower limits of this present study.

## Supplementary Statements

Commissioner Roy F. Bennett supports the majority of the recommendations in the *Report*, but urges alternative actions in several areas, including annualization and the cumulative employment account. On annualization, Bennett notes (correctly, in my view):

> The feasibility of the Annualization concept depends heavily on the adequacy of appropriate Income Supplementation plans which need to be developed. Without such plans, the Annualization concept would cause undue hardship to many individuals and impose a substantial strain on provincial welfare programs.[12]

---

[12]Ibid., p. 421.

Accordingly, Bennett recommends that, at least as an interim step, a one-for-one approach — one week of benefits for one week of work — be adopted up to some maximum, such as 30 weeks, with weekly benefits being determined at 60 percent or two-thirds of the average of the latest 13 weeks worked. Regional benefits would be phased out gradually, based on general economic conditions and on the success of the job creation and retraining programs outlined in the *Report*. This approach is fairly close to the proposals I outlined in Chapter 7 and to those that appear in Chapter 11.

In terms of the proposed cumulative employment account, Bennett is concerned about the inequities that could result between those who just meet the minimum 30-year working requirement and those who just fall short. Moreover, assistance might not be available for those older workers who have been working 30 years but have not met the minimum requirement because (a) they have worked abroad for a few years, (b) they had a period of self-employment, and (c) they had an average of less than 42 weeks of work per year. Bennett prefers that the entitlements be based simply on age, together with a minimum qualifying period in the labor force — 10 or 20 years. He recognizes that the viability of this proposal will hinge on, among other things, its acceptability under the Charter of Rights and Freedoms.

The supplementary statement by Commissioners F.J. Soboda and J.J. Munro is really an entirely separate report. Indeed, this supplementary report contains 77 recommendations, compared with 66 in the majority report. In many cases, particularly in terms of administration and operations, the recommendations of the two documents are fairly similar. However, the overall thrust of the Soboda-Munro supplementary is extremely critical of the general directions of the majority report. Operating from the premise that the existing program is "basically sound and needs only to be improved and strengthened,"[13] the authors offer the following proposals, among others, for improving UI:

- that the link between the duration of benefits and local unemployment rates be maintained (regionally extended benefits);
- that the minimum entrance requirement of ten weeks be extended to all classes of claimants, including those for sickness, maternity, and parental benefits;
- that the maximum benefit period be increased from 50 to 71 weeks;
- that the level of insurable earnings be established yearly at 125 percent of the eight-year moving average of earnings (instead of the current 100 percent);

---

[13]Ibid., p. 428.

- that the benefit rate be increased to 66 2/3 percent;
- that all pension income and severance and vacation pay be excluded from the definition of earnings for UI purposes;
- that the present exclusion from coverage of persons over age 65 be eliminated;
- that the maternity benefit period be 17 weeks, with the two-week waiting period being eliminated, and parental and adoption periods be 24 weeks;
- that part-time workers be eligible for UI if they have a minimum of six hours per week of regular employment;
- that the denial of benefits to workers involved in a strike be confined to workers actively on strike, and not extended to others who refuse to cross their picket lines.[14]

Clearly, these recommendations are way offside with respect to the three underlying challenges that have been discussed in the present study. In terms of the fiscal challenge alone, estimates by Commissioners Claude Forget and M.O. Morgan (in their own supplementary note) put the additional cost to UI of these proposals in the neighborhood of $3 billion.[15] And, as I argued in Chapter 7, the economic and sociodemographic challenges seem to point strongly to the need to rationalize UI, both in terms of its scope and its incentives. If Canadians were to agree to have a further $3 billion devoted to the social development envelope, the current UI program, in my view, surely would not be the place to spend it. I understand, however, that others hold different views on these matters.

## *Annualization: A Comparison with the Proposals in Chapter 7*

How do the Forget Commission's proposals for annualization compare with the proposals for UI reform I presented in Chapter 7? To recap, I proposed benefits based on 50 percent of average weekly insurable earnings, with the link between weeks worked and weeks of benefits determined as follows:

- one for one for the first 25 weeks;
- two weeks of work for each additional benefit week for weeks 26–51;
- three weeks of work for each further benefit week, up to the maximum of 52 benefit weeks.

---

[14]Ibid., pp. 470–477.
[15]Ibid., p. 419.

For presentation purposes, I refer to this as the "modified one-for-one approach".

By way of comparison, the following points are relevant:

• Neither approach discriminates by UI region either for benefit duration or for benefit payout.

• Both approaches ensure that benefits cannot exceed earnings over the requirement period. Annualization sets the replacement ratio at a constant 66 2/3 percent. The modified one-for-one approach sets the replacement ratio at 50 percent for the first 25 weeks, declining somewhat thereafter. The modified one-for-one approach offsets this to some degree, however, by having a lower tax-back rate — 50 percent, compared with 66 2/3 percent under annualization — on earnings while on claim.

• Both approaches effectively eliminate regional benefits; annualization does so indirectly through the approach to benefits, while the modified one-for-one approach does so directly.

• The real difference between the two approaches lies in their treatment of benefit levels for short-term workers. The modified one-for-one approach provides for identical weekly benefit rates for both long- and short-term workers — provided weekly insurable earnings are identical — but the number of benefit weeks is less for short-term workers. Annualization has identical benefit weeks but scales down weekly benefits quite dramatically for short-term employees.

• Annualization assumes that the appropriate settlement period is one year. The modified one-for-one approach assumes that it is the typical pay period. As I have already noted, under annualization, the reduced weekly income for short-term workers may help to deter such workers from voluntarily leaving the labor force. Under the modified one-for-one approach, the incentive for such workers to stay on is that after the benefit weeks run out, the payment falls to zero. In addition, a 50 percent tax-back rate is more likely than a 66 percent tax-back rate to encourage reentry into the labor force.

• One of the long-recognized roles of UI is to provide sufficient replacement income to allow job search while on claim. By maintaining weekly benefits, the modified one-for-one approach presumably fares much better on this score.

• The modified one-for-one approach appears to provide a more obvious transitional process — it simply phases out gradually the provisions for regional benefits, perhaps taking into account the concerns raised by Commissioner Bennett. Moreover, as Commissioner Bennett also noted, the modified one-for-one approach does not assume the presence of a comprehensive and integrated income support, income supplementation system. If and when such an income security is in place, annualization may well be a more appropriate approach.

It is important to focus not only on the differences between these two approaches but on their similarities as well. For example, both assume that the $3 billion currently allocated for regional extended benefits can be spent much more effectively, in terms of both income distribution grounds and longer-term enhancement for individuals and regions.

Perhaps the most important contribution of the Forget Commission is the fact that it forces Canadians to focus their attention on the manner in which unemployment insurance is, or ought to be, integrated with income support and income supplementation programs. If public discussion and debate become focused on this critical interrelationship, the Commission will have achieved its purpose, even if the annualization proposal does not become embodied in legislation.

Despite the several advantages of annualization, I still prefer the modified one-for-one approach. The following chapter summarizes the set of proposals for the welfare work subsystem, including the manner in which the modified one-for-one approach would be integrated into the subsystem.

# 11

## *Reform Proposals*

The reform proposals in this chapter are based on my belief that social policy in general and the welfare work subsystem in particular have to come to grips with the fiscal, economic, and sociodemographic challenges. To put the matter somewhat differently, social policy must become a more integral component of Canada's overall approach to the economic well-being of its citizens. Within this broad framework, however, there are several challenges that relate specifically to the operation of the welfare work subsystem:

• the adverse incentives arising from the fact that the UI program has moved away from its original function as an income insurance system and has taken on the features of a more general income support system;
• the confiscatory tax rates associated with the transition from welfare to work;
• the complexities of federal-provincial financial relations, particularly those arising from any major change in the UI regulations;
• the severe challenge on the employment front and the fact that monies supposedly earmarked for this purpose within UI could be more profitably spent in the context of specific job creation programs.

These challenges and concerns provide the backdrop for the reform proposals that follow.

### *UI and Job Creation*

The recommendations for UI reform given in Chapter 7 were broadly similar to those of the Macdonald Commission. A brief recapitulation of the Chapter 7 recommendations is in order here:

• Eligibility requirements should be uniform, with a qualifying period of not less than 15 weeks.
• Uniform provisions should apply for the duration of benefits, as follows: for the first 25 weeks, each week of work will generate one week of benefits; for weeks 26–51, each two weeks of work will generate one further week of benefits; for employment above 52 weeks, three weeks

of work will generate one week of benefits; the maximum benefit period is 52 weeks and would require 93 weeks of employment prior to a claim.
• The weekly benefit should be 50 percent of the average of the claimant's best 15 weeks of insured earnings over the qualifying period.
• The current 0–100 percent tax rate on income earned while on claim should be replaced by a uniform tax-back rate of 50 percent. The current accounting period for tax-back purposes is too short; it should be lengthened to at least one month and preferably to three months.
• The UI system should provide some additional ''adjustment funding'' for long-term employees who become unemployed, provided they undertake activities that increase their ability to become reemployed. These funds could take the form of either additional weeks of benefits or a higher scale of benefits for the regular benefit period. They would be earned at a rate of, say, two additional weeks of benefits or 2 percentage points of insured earnings for each year of continuous employment beyond the maximum 93-week qualifying period.
• Experience rating is desirable provided that it can be introduced in an administratively and economically feasible manner. Although the adoption of experience rating would move the system even more toward insurance principles, the removal of regional benefits from UI would do much to eliminate industry cross-subsidization and thus reduce the need for experience rating.
• The administrative structure of UI should be revamped to allow labor and business a much greater say in the operation of the program than they have at present.
• An annual adjustment in premiums to match benefits would lead to a procyclical policy of raising premium rates in periods of economic downswing. The UI system should either have access to the consolidated revenue fund or the ability to float its own debt so that premiums and benefits can be reconciled over the cycle rather than on an annual basis.

Although this approach clearly tilts the benefits of the system toward long-term employees, it is still quite generous to short-term workers. Moreover, even though regional benefits as such would be removed from UI, the distribution of benefits would still clearly favor high unemployment regions.

These proposals differ from those put forth by the Macdonald Commission in several respects. First, they incorporate some reward, in the form of additional UI benefits, for long-service employees who, while unemployed, are willing to undertake employment-enhancing activities. This provision would allow the TAAP-type program described below to focus on employment creation and adjustment enhancement for *all* Canadians. Hence, these functions would be separated conceptually and operationally from UI.

The second area of difference relates to the tax-back rate. Under the scheme outlined above, workers would always have an incentive to reenter the labor market: the value of their UI benefits would fall to zero once they found employment that generated an income equal to the insurable earnings on which their benefits were based. Actually, the Macdonald Commission's proposals do provide for a tax-back rate of sorts. Given the UISP scheme, benefits from UI presumably would be viewed as employment income and would be offset — at a 20 percent tax rate — against the guaranteed income level. However, this aspect of the interaction between UI and UISP probably would be perverse — the low tax-back rate incorporated in UISP might well simply reproduce the existing situation, which encourages short-term or seasonal employment.

Finally, the Macdonald Commission is silent on the issue of greater labor-business participation in the running of UI.

Naturally, there are many issues that these broad recommendations do not touch on, such as the waiting period for benefits, the carryover of credits for claimants who find work before they exhaust their benefits, and the trigger point for the coverage of part-time workers. These and many similar considerations are clearly important, but it would not be productive in the present context to focus on this level of detail. The key to reform is obviously to come to some consensus about the features of the grand design. Once this design has been determined, the detailed regulations will fall into place.

There is, however, one further important issue, namely, the phase-in or transition period. Since the scheme proposed here focuses on changing the duration of benefits — reducing it for short-term workers and lengthening it, at least in some cases, for long-term workers — the provisions probably should be introduced gradually over, say, a five-year period. However, the scaling down of benefits to 50 percent of insurable earnings from 60 percent and the incentive-oriented 50 percent tax-back rate probably could be introduced more quickly.

## Job Creation and Adjustment Enhancement

Since the proposal for UI reform outlined here would generate substantial savings, the next issue is what should be done with these savings. Conveniently, the bulk of the savings would arise because the benefits for fishermen and the regional extended benefits would be removed from the program. Since these benefits are not currently paid for out of premium income, this facilitates the transfer of these noninsurance aspects of UI into more appropriate departments and programs.

Obviously, since the fishing benefits component of UI is targeted to a specific group, both regionally and industrially, some transitional mechanisms would have to be put in place immediately on dropping this component from UI. At one extreme, of course, the benefits could be maintained for a while under the present operating procedures, but placed within a different program or department. The difficulty, politically, with such an approach is that the substantial subsidy to the fishing industry would then be out in the open, as it were. But this is exactly what should occur. Canadians surely realize that it would be intolerable simply to curtail, cold turkey, the funds directed to this industry. Hence, they would likely be quite tolerant of a generous transition program that would have as its goal the rationalization of the industry. There have already been several studies along these lines, so the problem is not one of coming up with alternatives. What is needed, rather, is the courage to bite the bullet; a rationalization of the UI program would provide an appropriate context for this step to be taken.

Some of the savings that would arise from the effective removal of regional extended benefits clearly should be funneled back into the system in a combination of job creation programs and programs that enhance the ability of the disadvantaged to pursue gainful employment. As I noted in Chapter 7, despite the fact that these benefits are called "regional" benefits, they no longer go merely to claimants in the have-not provinces. The rise in unemployment rates across the country has meant that all but a handful of the 48 designated UI regions now qualify for regional benefits. Thus, what effectively triggers these "regional" benefits is the national unemployment rate, not disparities in unemployment rates across the regions. In other words, the spending essentially plays a *stabilization role* within UI. As the national unemployment rate falls, the "regional" benefits component falls.

Hence, as long as unemployment rates remained high, the federal government could not in good conscience merely pocket all the savings that would result from the proposed reorganization of UI. The availability of these savings, plus the fact that UI is a very poor instrument for creating employment, would provide the rationale for a TAAP-type ancilliary program. Initially, at least, a program of this kind probably should make some concessions to the existing geographical distribution of regional benefits.

I have no special insights about how the funds would best be spent. Given the rather poor record of past job creation and skill-enhancing programs, however, some of the emphasis probably should be on experimentation and innovation. Skill and literacy upgrading, wage subsidies for apprentice-type activities, and even community-based projects could well be part of the overall package. Since the new UI program could be phased in gradually, this TAAP-type job creation program should also have modest beginnings and should be subject to periodic, independent evaluation.

Actually, even these proposals for regional job creation should be viewed as temporary. It seems reasonably clear that once this round of social policy and tax policy reform is completed, pressures will begin to build toward instituting a full-blown, income-tested guaranteed annual income. In this context, some of the UI savings eventually would be earmarked for funding the GAI. Presumably, this would apply to job creation programs as well. In an earlier chapter, I suggested that Newfoundland might provide an ideal place in which to experiment with such a GAI system, perhaps following the recommendations of the Newfoundland Royal Commission on Employment and Unemployment.

There is one other related area where new initiatives may be warranted. Canadians are used to tax-assisted devices for retirement savings, for purchasing their first home, and, in Quebec, for purchasing new equity issues. Equivalent programs ought to exist for mid-career skill enhancement — particularly in the context of a rapidly changing economy where skill obsolescence is increasingly a concern. Surely it is not inappropriate to place the need for retraining on an equal tax footing with the purchase of a first home. The suggestion is not novel. A proposal for a Registered Education and Training Savings Plan appeared in the 1981 report of the Task Force on Labour Market Development.[1] Indeed, one might go even further. I have always found it a bit ironic that long-service workers who become unemployed have frequently built up adequate retirement income credits, although their far more pressing need is for *current* income. Under certain circumstances, it would be reasonable to allow people in this position to "borrow" from the retirement fund in order to enhance their ability for reemployment. This arrangement would increase not only their current income but, presumably, also their retirement income. To be sure, one would have to take care in deciding how such a system would operate, probably even to the point of requiring some performance standards such as the successful completion of the training program. Nonetheless, it is probably an idea whose time has come.

In summary, then, this part of the package of recommendations is designed to rectify some of the following more glaring deficiencies in the current system:

• the excessive rewards to short-term labor attachment;
• the encouragement of temporary employment and unstable employment patterns;

[1]Canada, Task Force on Labour Market Development, *Labour Market Development in the 1980s* (Ottawa: Supply and Services Canada, 1981).

- the anti-adjustment bias that results from longer benefit eligibility in regions where the likelihood of finding a job is low;
- the horizontal inequities resulting from the fact that UI treats otherwise identical individuals differently on the basis of their places of residence;
- the adverse effect on reentry associated with the zero percent tax rate on earnings up to the first 25 percent of benefits and the confiscatory (100 percent) tax on additional earnings up to the maximum benefit level;
- the growing recognition that the noninsurance goals served by UI could be accomplished far more effectively if they were transferred to more appropriate programs; and
- the equally growing recognition that something is seriously wrong with a system that, in effect, pays out over $11 billion a year in order to compensate individuals for not working.

It is important to remember that UI and its problems are inseparable from the welfare work subsystem as a whole, and that any changes in UI would also have an impact on the subsystem's other components. It is to these components that I now turn.

### *The Family Benefits Package*

My discussion of the Macdonald Commission's proposed UISP program made it clear that I have serious misgivings about jumping immediately into a comprehensive GAI approach to income support. These misgivings would remain even if the tax-back rate on earnings within UISP were set at 50 percent rather than 20 percent. An incremental approach would ensure that we made no "big" mistakes, but even apart from this consideration, it is the preferable approach to take. Canada's current welfare system and family benefits package serves such a multitude of purposes and clients that it is not yet amenable to being subsumed into one grandiose GAI design. Incrementalism allows one to address those aspects of the current system where the pressures for reform are the greatest. With this said, however, it is imperative that incrementalism not lose sight of the overall goals addressed by both the UISP program and the Quebec White Paper.

### *A Menu of Alternatives*

The range of alternative approaches to the reform of the family benefits package depends critically on the degree to which Canada is committed to overall tax reform. Thus, the proposals that follow become progressively more ambitious as the degree of tax reform increases.

No Tax Reform

First of all, if very little or no tax reform takes place, very little in the way of family benefits reform can be expected either. The ongoing implementation of the measures announced in the 1985 federal budget will result in an enhanced targeting of these benefits, however, and one possibility would be to keep the process going. For example, once the child tax exemption falls to the level of family allowances, the value of these two programs can be frozen, or even reduced gradually. Some of the savings then can be diverted to enhancing the refundable child tax credit, with the remainder used for such purposes as marginal rate reductions or financing new requirements on the social policy front. While such initiatives are desirable, they fall more in the realm of tinkering than reform.

Moreover, as the value of the income-tested refundable tax credit is enhanced, it becomes increasingly important to focus on the characteristics of this program. Currently, this tax credit is worth $454 per child. The phasing out of the credit begins only after the family's net income exceeds $23,500. Thereafter, the credit decreases by $5 for each additional $100 of income — that is, the value credit for a single child is exhausted when net income is $9,100 above the $23,500 threshold, or $32,600. For a family with two children, the break-even level is $41,700; for a family with three it is $50,800. This is far too generous a tax-back scheme. Ironically, while the switch from child tax exemptions to refundable child tax credits increases the progressivity of the tax system, the situation is arising where the *child tax credit itself is not sufficiently targeted*. In my view, the appropriate approach to the income-tested tax credit is to scale down rather dramatically both the threshold and break-even levels. Suppose, for illustrative purposes, that the tax-back rate began to take effect at a family net income level of $12,500. Suppose further that the tax-back rate were set at $7.50 per $100 of additional net income. Under this scenario, a two-child family would exhaust its credits with a net income of roughly $24,500. This would generate substantial fiscal savings, part of which might well go into enriching the tax credit. But if the tax credit is enriched, the tax-back rate should increase, leaving both the threshold and break-even levels unchanged.

There are at least two reasons, however, why such a proposal would be a tough sell politically. The first relates to the fact that it would represent a tax increase for the beleaguered middle class. This arises primarily because we are discussing a no-tax-reform scenario. Middle-income Canadians could be satisfied if, in turn for these reduced tax credits, they faced a lower marginal tax rate. It is in this important sense that meaningful reform of the family benefits package depends on the overall commitment to general tax reform.

The second reason relates more to perception than to reality. It has become traditional in Canada to assess the equity of the personal income tax system by the number of individuals or families that are not required to file a tax return. Almost by definition, a budget that drops several thousand families off the tax rolls is billed as a progressive initiative. From a "targeting" or GAI perspective, this is completely wrong. The way to improve the economic well-being of the disadvantaged is, first, to increase the income guarantee levels but, then, to begin to tax earned income at a low threshold level, always ensuring of course that the tax rate does not come close to being confiscatory. Even though the thrust of my analysis is that Canada is not yet ready for a full-blown NIT or GAI, the time has come to initiate certain programs that have the targeting and incentive features that are characteristic of negative income taxation. These comments are probably as relevant to the operations of provincial welfare systems as they are to the reform of the federal family benefits system.

### A BTT or VAT with Lower PIT Rates, but No PIT Reform

The second tax reform scenario would incorporate a shift from taxing income to taxing consumption — through a BTT or VAT — and, thus, lower PIT rates, but with no substantial reform of the personal income tax system itself. This is the minimum reform needed to satisfy the economic challenge — that is, to prevent the movement of labor and capital to the United States in response to lower U.S. marginal income tax rates. However, it also enhances substantially the ability of the system to initiate significant measures on the family benefits front.

First, it now becomes possible to increase the selectivity of the income-tested child tax credit. Middle-income families will lose some of their current benefits, but as compensation they will be subject to a lower marginal PIT rate. This is really the essence of enhanced targeting and where the payoffs of greater selectivity become sizable.

Second, the refundable BTT or VAT low-income tax credit — which I assume is an integral ingredient of any consumption tax in order to reduce its regressivity — will represent a sea change in Canada's tax system, since the concept of income-tested refundable tax credits will be extended in a meaningful way to adults for the first time. Not only will this have significant implications for the operations of provincial welfare systems (as will be elaborated in the next section) but it will also be a key element in any future move in the direction of establishing an income-tested GAI.

### A BTT or VAT and PIT Reform

The ideal scenario is full PIT reform, in the context of a shift from taxing income to taxing consumption. In addition to the lowering of marginal rates made possible by a greater reliance on consumption taxes, further PIT rate reductions would arise from the combination of base broadening and the conversion of tax exemptions to tax credits. Under this scenario, the following sorts of initiatives are possible:

- a lowering and flattening of the marginal tax rate structure, which, for example, will serve to minimize the after-tax differences across income classes for tax exemptions such as RRSP and registered pension deductions;
- a shift from exemptions to credits, which will further increase the progressivity of the system — although, to the extent that the marginal rate structure becomes flatter, the difference between exemptions and credits is reduced;
- a move to make some of those credits refundable and income tested — that is, a move toward an income-tested GAI;
- a substantial increase in the degree of targeting of income-tested refundable credits, made possible by a significant lowering of marginal rates; and
- a much better integration of the negative and positive income tax systems.

This last point is particularly noteworthy. In essence, it implies that the income level at which the tax-back rate exhausts the value of refundable tax credits is also the income level at which the positive side of the income tax system begins to take effect. In the limit, one could even imagine that the tax-back rate on any refundable credits would equal the marginal tax rate once the positive income tax system began to apply.

Under this comprehensive reform scenario, all three underlying challenges can be addressed. The enhanced targeting of social benefits can free up valuable resources that, in turn, can be used for marginal rate deductions. Lower marginal tax rates and enhanced incentives within the social programs — for labor force reentry, for example — will contribute to meeting the economic challenge. Less directly affected is the sociodemographic challenge. But even here, some strides can be made. For example, integrating any BTT low-income tax credit with the GIS can generate savings, some of which, in turn, can be used to meet the challenge of the aging of the population.

## *The Welfare System*

Reform of the family benefits package can have substantial implications for the operations of provincial welfare systems. Increased reliance on refundable tax credits and particularly the existence of a low-income

BTT credit imply that the federal government will be transferring more income to Canadians who currently find themselves on welfare. This is a desirable outcome for several reasons.

First, the interregional adjustment process would argue for a greater federal role in funding welfare on both efficiency and equity grounds. Differences in economic performance among Canada's regions mean that workers move from provinces whose economies are stagnant to provinces that are growing. When adversity strikes, however, many of these workers migrate back to their provinces of origin, exhaust their UI payments, and fall onto the welfare rolls. To the extent that welfare spending in some provinces is triggered by economic adjustment forces beyond their borders, there are externality arguments in favor of a larger federal funding presence.

Second, the reform of UI may imply an increased recourse to welfare in some provinces, even if more of the savings go to job creation or skill enhancement policies in the affected regions. A larger federal share of welfare expenditures — through enhanced family benefits — may be necessary in order to obtain any meaningful UI reform.

Third, and most important from the perspective of the evolution of the welfare system, family benefits reform will facilitate incentive-oriented approaches to welfare design. As noted earlier, four provinces already have some form of supplementary income-tested benefits for the working poor. Together with any new federal income-tested refundable tax credits, these measures will go a considerable way to ensure that the overall tax rate in the transition from welfare to work no longer nears being confiscatory. Moreover, the stage would be set for provinces to begin, or to enlarge on, income testing for some expenditure programs, such as housing subsidies and medical premium relief. Indeed, it is even possible to imagine the provinces taking a major step toward integrating their welfare systems into the personal income tax delivery system. Suppose, for example, that in tax reform, the federal government were to follow the Ontario Economic Council's recommendation for a "tax on base" rather than a "tax on tax" as part of the shared federal-provincial PIT system.[2] What this would mean is that the provinces would be able to apply their own rate and bracket structures to the common tax base; under the current system, they are restricted to applying a single tax rate to the federal basic tax. Under this scenario, the scope for income testing of provincial welfare payments increases substantially.

To be sure, there will be some hurdles to be overcome in all of this. For example, if the federal government does increase its payments to low-income Canadian families, it may desire some *quid quo pro* from the

---

[2]Ontario Economic Council, *A Separate Personal Income Tax for Ontario*, Ontario Economic Council Position Paper (Toronto, 1983), p. 164.

provinces — for example, a reduction in other payments, such as transfers for the established programs or a reduction in its formula-related CAP payments. Moreover, while one would hope that the federal government would encourage provincial initiatives in the welfare area, one would also hope that Ottawa would ensure that such initiatives did not embody such features as residency requirements, which serve to inhibit mobility and, more generally, fragment the internal common market. However, there are also opportunities for increased cooperation and coordination. Federal-provincial consultation could lead to more uniformity in the rules that govern welfare eligibility across provinces. There is also scope for joint efforts in the areas of job creation and retraining, particularly if these are related to a gradual phasing out of regional benefits under UI. Finally, any increased flexibility or decentralization of the activities of the Canada Employment Centres probably could only be achieved through federal-provincial interaction.

## Conclusion

This completes the overview of suggested reforms relating to the welfare work system. The analysis now shifts to the established programs subsystem and the equalization subsystem. Although these subsystems are clearly integral to overall social policy reform, they lie somewhat apart from the federal government's ongoing commitment to social policy reform. Some readers may want to proceed directly to the concluding chapter, "Agenda for Reform".

# PART IV

## The Established Programs Subsystem

# 12

## *The Status Quo*

### *Introduction*

If federal-provincial interactions loom large in the welfare work and retirement subsystems, they come close to dominating the public discussion of programs in the areas of health and postsecondary education — commonly called the "established programs". The reasons for this are rather obvious. Although both health and postsecondary education are under provincial jurisdiction,[1] a very substantial component of the funding for programs in these areas comes from the federal government. Given the high profile of these programs and the fact that together they affect the lives of every Canadian, it is hardly surprising that the federal government is generally at pains to make its role as visible as possible and to link its cash transfers to "accountability" to Parliament. Even without efforts of this kind, transfers as large as those associated with health and postsecondary education inevitably would be drawn into the fiscal restraint debate in these times of mushrooming deficits.

As Table 18 shows, federal cash transfers in fiscal year 1983–84 for the established programs totaled $7.6 billion; a further $5.2 billion arose from tax point transfers, for an overall total of $13.8 billion. This figure would be larger still if the table included the equalization payments associated with these tax points. Clearly, Ottawa has a very substantial financial presence in the operations of the established programs.

Nevertheless, many of the provinces probably would challenge the interpretation in Table 18 of Ottawa's contributions to the established programs — a circumstance that illustrates the strenuousness of the federal-provincial tug-of-war in this area. For one thing, several provinces would claim that the breakdown of the cash component between health and postsecondary education is inappropriate, since from 1977 onward the federal financing for these programs has been unconditional. The very nature of an unconditional grant is that there should be no monitoring of how monies transferred are allocated either between health and postsecondary education or between the established programs and other provincial spending priorities. Furthermore, many provinces view the tax

---

[1]It is probably correct to say that the federal government has never conceded that the responsibility for the "research" component of postsecondary education belongs to the provinces under the Constitution.

**Table 18**
**Estimated Federal Transfers Relating to**
**Established Programs, fiscal year 1983–84**
*($ millions)*

| Program | Transfers |
|---|---|
| *Cash grants* | |
| Hospital insurance | 3,439.9 |
| Medicare | 1,184.3 |
| Extended health care | 939.5 |
| Postsecondary education | 2,068.8 |
| Subtotal | 7,632.5 |
| *Tax transfers* | |
| 13.5 Personal income tax points[a] | 4,954.5 |
| 1.0 Corporate income tax points[a] | 275.8 |
| Subtotal | 5,230.3 |
| *Total* | *12,862.8* |

[a]These tax points are equalized under the equalization program. The totals shown here, however, are net of this equalization.

Source: Royal Commission on the Economic Union and Development Prospects for Canada, *Report*, vol. 3 (Ottawa: Supply and Services Canada, 1985), Table 22-13.

point component as part of their own-source revenue and not as a "transfer" of funds from the federal government. Indeed, the funding arrangements for Quebec raise doubts about the "federal" nature of even the cash component. In lieu of cash transfers, Quebec receives additional tax point transfers. In effect, this means that Canadians with identical incomes and family status pay less federal income tax in Quebec than elsewhere in Canada but more provincial income tax. As a rough rule of thumb, the allocation of personal income taxes in Ontario is two-thirds to Ottawa and one-third to the province. In Quebec, the allocation is closer to fifty-fifty, although to some extent this distribution reflects the fact that the overall income tax bill, federal and provincial, is higher in Quebec. The other provinces turned down the offer to follow Quebec in opting out of the cash transfer component. Nonetheless, the result is that it is difficult for Ottawa to maintain that these cash payments represent a federal transfer rather than a provincial source of revenue, given that, for Quebec, they have been converted into a tax point transfer.

Despite all of this, the fact remains that federal "funding" for the established programs came into being as a result of federal legislation that draws on the federal government's spending power under the Constitution. Hence, in principle at least, the funding provisions can be altered by an act of Parliament without the consent of the provinces.

Thus, although the object here is to focus on the relationship between the established programs and the three challenges that underlie the overall analysis of social policy, it is probably inevitable that on occasion the discussion will appear to "take sides". It is probably impossible to present even a description, let alone an interpretation, of the evolution of the established programs without making champions of one level of government or the other. Moreover, when the discussion comes to recommendations relating to the equity, efficiency, and the fiscal dimensions of these programs, it will, in effect, take a position on the federal-provincial overlap. Nonetheless, my intention is to stay as clear of the intergovernmental issue as I can and to direct attention instead to the programs themselves and how they are serving Canadians.

To anticipate the recommendations somewhat, a priority for the evolution of the health care system is to establish a degree of operational flexibility sufficient to ensure that the provinces can capitalize on any potential efficiencies in the delivery of health care. For postsecondary education, the priority is to recognize, more than we do at present, that university education and, particularly, university research are likely to be absolutely critical to Canada's future economic development. In this respect, postsecondary education is as much a cornerstone of economic policy as it is of social policy. If Canada is to achieve these goals, however, it is absolutely imperative that Ottawa and the provinces not let jurisdictional or fiscal squabbles dominate the appropriate evolution of the established programs. The stakes are simply too high.

The discussion of the established programs proceeds as follows. The remainder of the present chapter provides a brief overview of the recent evolution of these programs. Chapter 13 focuses on health and advances proposals for reform in this area. Chapter 14 discusses postsecondary education and the pertinent proposals for reform; it also provides a brief summary of the subsystem as a whole.

## The Evolution of the Established Programs

Before 1977, the federal government provided funding for health and postsecondary education on a shared-cost, open-ended basis. The federal share was roughly 50 percent, although the manner in which the monies were allocated to the provinces varied by program. The 1977 fiscal arrangements abandoned cost sharing for an unconditional, block-funding scheme. Future transfers to the provinces would not be determined by program expenditures but, rather, would increase annually in accordance with GNP growth. The precise funding details were complex, incorporating both income tax point transfers and cash transfers; an additional sum was thrown in as compensation for the termination of the so-called revenue guarantee.[2]

Both Ottawa and the provinces welcomed the 1977 initiative. The prevailing view was that the program specific, shared cost approach encouraged overspending, since the provinces, in effect, were spending 50-cent dollars. The federal government disliked the open-ended nature of the cost-sharing scheme, since it meant that a significant portion of the federal budget was determined by spending decisions made in the ten provincial capitals. The provinces objected in particular to the treatment of health services under the old approach: efforts to increase efficiency by substituting paramedics for doctors in certain areas or by resorting to convalescent homes rather than hospitals were effectively thwarted because the cost-sharing provisions did not cover these activities. All in all, both sides welcomed the new arrangements.

It is not quite correct to say that there were no conditions associated with the transfers. Although the provinces could use the funds they assigned to postsecondary education as they pleased, for funds devoted to health programs the existing principles continued to apply — comprehensiveness, universality, accessibility, portability, and the administration of the plan by either public agencies or other agencies on a nonprofit basis.

The honeymoon that followed the introduction of the new arrangements soon ended. Only a year later, the federal government asked the provinces to accept a lower escalation of the transfers as part of an overall federal program of fiscal restraint. The provinces refused, as was their right under the 1977 provisions. In the deliberations leading up to the 1982 renegotiations of the fiscal arrangements, however, the federal government proposed to remove from the financing package the compensation for the loss of the revenue guarantee. This and other issues led to the televised confrontation between the premiers and the prime minister at the February 1982 First Ministers' Conference — surely one of the most controversial on record. In the end, the federal position prevailed, with the result that over the 1982–87 fiscal arrangements cycle, transfers to the provinces were some $6 billion less than they would have been had the existing arrangements been extended.

The next move occurred when the federal government placed the postsecondary education component of the transfer under the provisions of the federal "6 and 5" program, a move that reduced payments by an estimated $118 million in fiscal year 1983–84 and $260 million in fiscal

---

[2]The revenue guarantee began as a temporary program to compensate the provinces for allowing their income tax systems to incorporate the federal reform measures introduced in the early 1970s. By 1977, the program involved payments to the provinces of nearly $1 billion. Partial compensation for the termination of the revenue guarantee was folded into the 1977 block-funding arrangements for established programs financing.

year 1984–85. At about the same time, several of the provinces — presumably because of the reduction in the growth of the grants and the fiscal impact of the recession — began to pass on some of the costs of funding the established programs to their citizens. Thus, some provinces began to allow extra billing for health services. The federal government's response was the 1984 *Canada Health Act.*

Despite the fact that all federal parties supported the act, it was a very controversial piece of legislation. The controversy arose in part because the act was every bit as much about federal-provincial fiscal relations as it was about health. For some of the provinces, but obviously not all of them, the provisions of the act confirmed their worst fears. In their view, the act:

• defined in part what ought to be covered under the provincial programs;
• effectively eliminated extra billing as a source of funding;
• called into question some previously accepted means of funding medicare, such as medicare premiums;
• made it more difficult for the provinces to legislate fee schedules for doctors, since the latter had access to appeal procedures;
• was open-ended and unilateral, since its provisions could be altered by Parliament.

The other side of the coin is that the federal government viewed the legislation as essential to the saving of medicare. And it must be agreed that Ottawa was supported in this initiative by the majority — perhaps the vast majority — of Canadians. The following chapter has more to say on this issue.

More recently, the focus has been on postsecondary education. Ottawa argues that the provinces are diverting the federal transfers associated with postsecondary education into other spending areas — even to the point, in some cases, of spending less overall on postsecondary education than they receive for this purpose from the federal government. Table 19 illustrates this concern by comparing data for fiscal years 1977–78 and 1984–85. Although these data exclude other sources of funding for postsecondary education, such as tuition fees and private sources of revenue, they clearly support the federal government's contention. Column 3 of the table indicates that, in all provinces, the provincial share of overall funding for postsecondary education has fallen, in some cases quite dramatically.

On the other hand, as Table 20 shows, in the case of funding for health programs, it is the federal share that has fallen. Moreover, because the current growth of health care expenditures is rapidly outstripping the GNP

**Table 19**
*Established Programs Financing and Postsecondary
Education Transfers, fiscal years 1977–78 and 1984–85*

|  | Transfers[a] | | Increase in fiscal transfer "share" or reduction in "purely provincial share" |
|---|---|---|---|
|  | 1977–78 | 1984–85 |  |
| Newfoundland | 83.3% | 106.9% | 23.6% |
| Prince Edward Island | 101.5 | 106.9 | 5.3 |
| Nova Scotia | 87.5 | 91.6 | 4.1 |
| New Brunswick | 98.1 | 101.8 | 3.7 |
| Quebec | 56.1 | 59.6 | 3.5 |
| Ontario | 73.7 | 88.7 | 15.0 |
| Manitoba | 80.3 | 102.9 | 22.5 |
| Saskatchewan | 81.6 | 90.3 | 8.7 |
| Alberta | 63.9 | 73.1 | 9.2 |
| British Columbia | 78.9 | 104.3 | 25.4 |
| *Canada* | *68.9* | *79.6* | *10.7* |

[a]As a percentage of provincial operating grants to universities and colleges.

Source: A.W. Johnson, *Giving Greater Point and Purpose to the Federal Financing of Post-Secondary Education and Research in Canada* (Ottawa: Secretary of State, 1985), p. 12.

growth rate, the federal share would register further declines if Table 20 incorporated data for more recent years. Given that overall expenditures on health exceed, by a considerable margin, those on postsecondary education, it may well be that the provincial share of total funding for the established programs has increased since the advent of block funding in fiscal year 1977–78.

The provinces would argue that all of these ratios are irrelevant, since the essence of unconditional grants is that the provinces can spend the money as they wish. And the federal government presumably would counter by insisting that the transfer of such large amounts of money to the provinces requires some federal accountability with respect to how these funds are spent. And on and on.

The purpose of this brief and, one hopes, even-handed description of the evolution of established program funding over the past decade or so has been to provide the necessary background for an analysis of the challenges that face both the health and postsecondary education sectors. Whether one favors the federal or the provincial view of these issues, however, the time has certainly come for statesmanship to prevail: it is essential that the federal and provincial governments find approaches to federal-provincial financing that are consistent with ensuring that the

**Table 20**
*Health Care Expenditures, fiscal years 1977–78 to 1982–83*

|  | Federal government contributions to health care ($ millions) | Provincial & local government health expenditures ($ millions) | Percentage of federal contribution |
|---|---|---|---|
| 1977–78 | $4,673 | $10,900 | 42.9% |
| 1978–79 | 5,343 | 12,124 | 44.1 |
| 1979–80 | 6,094 | 13,536 | 45.0 |
| 1980–81 | 6,814 | 15,723 | 43.3 |
| 1981–82 | 7,631 | 18,596 | 41.0 |
| 1982–83 | 8,512 | 21,521 | 39.6 |

Sources: The figures in column 1 are from Government of Canada, *Preserving Universal Medicare* (Ottawa: Supply and Services Canada, 1983), p. 29; the figures in column 2 are from "Federal Proposal to Reduce Health and Post-Secondary Education Financing" (Statement by Provincial Ministers of Finance and Treasurers, April 1983), Table 3.

design of the established programs meets the fiscal, economic, and sociodemographic challenges underpinning the future of the social programs.

# 13

## Health Care

### The Challenges

There is little doubt that Canadians take immense pride in their publicly funded health care system. Indeed, there is a fear (whether founded or not) that any free trade deal with the United States would force Canadians to abandon their social programs and, in particular, medicare. As Figure 2 indicates, the first decade of the full-blown public health care system in Canada — roughly the decade of the 1970s — saw health expenditures level off as a percentage of GNP, in sharp contrast with trends south of the border.

Delicate as the subject is, however, the thrust of this chapter is that all is not well with Canada's health care system. If the costs of the system were managable for a decade or so, the last few years have seen them rise dramatically. In Ontario, for example, health expenditures accounted for 28.5 cents of the Ontario expenditure dollar in fiscal year 1981–82. By fiscal year 1984–85, the figure had risen to 30.9 cents.[1] In absolute terms, Ontario health care expenditures increased by 58 percent during this period. The cost pressures in other provinces are roughly similar.

With health care accounting for about 30 percent of provincial expenditures, it is not surprising that the provinces increasingly are concerned about the potential for further cost escalation and about the impact of rising health care costs, in a period of overall fiscal pressure, on the levels of expenditure on *other* provincial priorities, including postsecondary education. The situation is particularly worrisome for provinces that are in the process of eliminating extra billing, since the *quid quo pro* expected by the medical profession is an increase in the fee schedule. All of the provinces are concerned about the rise in costs associated with the aging of the population and the development of increasingly expensive diagnostic and treatment procedures, full access to which consumers expect as an integral part of the medicare system.

The challenge, therefore, is to rationalize the delivery systems, particularly in light of the aging of the population, while recognizing that Canadians value highly the basic features of the overall system. In a recent

---

[1]Robert F. Nixon, *1985 Ontario Budget* (Toronto: Ministry of Treasury and Economics, 1985), Chart C2.

**Figure 2**
*Canadian and U.S. Health Expenditures, 1960-82*
*(as a percentage of GNP)*

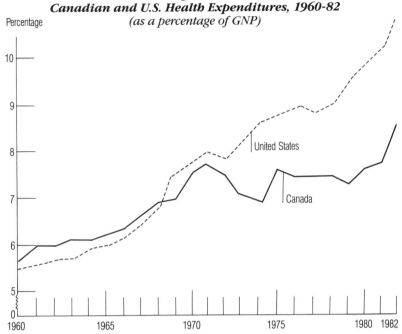

Note: Canadian data for 1981 and 1982 are provisional.

Source: Greg L. Stoddart, "Rationalizing the Health-Care System," in Thomas J. Courchene, David W. Conklin, and Gail C.A. Cook, eds., *Ottawa and the Provinces: The Distribution of Money and Power,* vol. 2 (Toronto: Ontario Economic Council, 1985), p. 12.

overview of the health care area, Greg Stoddart suggests that meeting this challenge will be a tall order, for the following reasons:

— Those responsible for providing and administering the provision of specific health services to patients exert steady pressure on government to increase its resource commitments in order to maintain existing styles of delivery, existing incomes, or both.
— The main policy instruments currently available to or at least employed by government for accomplishing change are relatively blunt fiscal measures (such as making decisions on fee levels and budgets and setting controls on the number of providers and hospital beds) backed only by a willingness to engage in confrontation.
— The sheer size of governments' financial commitments to existing programs severely limits the funds available for innovation

or experimentation with alternative financing and delivery arrangements, even if they are potentially more cost-effective.
— The health-care system itself has few internal adjustment or equilibrating mechanisms to effect the reallocation of existing budgets to improve efficiency.
— Perhaps most important, no consensus exists among the system's numerous actors as to which trade-offs and reallocations might be in the public interest. This lack of agreement is not surprising considering that all the key actors — providers, administrators, patients, and bureaucrats — are behaving quite rationally, given their legitimate concerns for their own welfare, the performance expectations imposed upon them, and the incentives they face.[2]

Stoddart summarizes the situation as follows:

Given this environment, the surprise is not that inefficient patterns of resource allocations exist, but that they are not worse; not that global expenditure-control is now becoming extremely difficult and confrontational, but that it has lasted this long. The lid stayed on so long at least in part because the health-care system is operated and utilized by dedicated professionals and conscientious consumers who do understand that resources are not infinite. Unfortunately, they are given few mechanisms or incentives for aligning their own goals and welfare with the social goal of efficiency.[3]

What mechanisms and/or incentives might enhance the efficiency of health care delivery? The next section presents a range of alternatives to the present delivery system. Although the object of all of these alternatives is to provide incentives and encourage competition, the intention here is *not* to suggest that Canada's health system be privatized. Along with the overwhelming majority of Canadians, I support the publicly funded, publicly monitored nature of the health care system. Rather, my purpose is to suggest ways in which to enhance the roles of competition, efficiency, and incentives *within* the existing public system.

### Prospects for Rationalization

What follows is a discussion of several possible approaches to the problem of rationalizing the health care system. This discussion is intended

---

[2]Greg L. Stoddart, "Rationalizing the Health-Care System," in Thomas J. Courchene, David W. Conklin, and Gail C.A. Cook, eds., *Ottawa and the Provinces: The Distribution of Money and Power*, vol. 2 (Toronto: Ontario Economic Council, 1985), pp. 6–7.
[3]Ibid., p. 20.

to be suggestive rather than exhaustive. Many of the approaches are followed in other jurisdictions and some are followed in the various provinces. What is rather exciting, however, is the fact, that with ten separate provincial health care systems, different approaches can be implemented at the same time. This ability to experiment in the various provinces is absolutely critical in terms of finding more efficient approaches to health care delivery.

### Payment Mechanisms

The prevailing system is based on the concept of solo practitioners, with fee for service as the method of physician payment. One objection to the fee for service approach is that it provides incentives for the oversupply of services; it is difficult, however, to introduce alternative payment mechanisms within the solo practitioner framework. The situation is different elsewhere. The United States, for example, has seen a very rapid proliferation of so-called health maintenance organizations (HMOs), which provide service on a "capitation" basis. Under this system, an individual or family pays a lump sum fee to an HMO in return for full medical coverage — under a public system, this fee presumably would be paid by the government. In 1980, there were 244 HMOs in the United States. By 1985, there were 480. In terms of numbers of members, the expansion was equally dramatic — from under 10 million in 1980 to over 20 million in 1985.[4]

The incentives under a capitation system are obviously very different from those that operate under a fee for service system. Since the physician group does not increase its income by offering greater services, there is an incentive to ensure that the clients remain healthy. Critics can argue, of course, that under an HMO arrangement, physicians have an incentive to save money at the expense of patient treatment. Were this actually the case, however, it is most unlikely that the number of HMOs in the United States would have doubled over the past five years.

There is a further difference between an HMO system and a fee for services system. Although it is perhaps impolitic to raise this point, there can be little doubt that, under the latter system, the fee schedule itself plays an important role in determining the method of treatment. Indeed, one rationale for extra billing is that it can correct anomalies in the fee schedule. (I am not asserting that this is the most important aspect of extra billing, only that it is an aspect.) In any event, influences of this kind are absent in an HMO setting.

---

[4]Jennifer Hull, "Physicians organize to stop HMOs from altering practice of medicine," *Wall Street Journal*, June 23, 1986, p. 23.

Since the solo practitioner, fee for service approach is so well entrenched in Canada, any change would have to be a gradual one. Ontario now has one capitation-based "health service organization", located in Sault Ste. Marie. As Stoddart notes:

> Evaluations of its performance, contrasted with that of fee-for-service physicians in Sault Ste. Marie, have consistently indicated that capitation arrangements can lower health-care costs, even though the clinic's full potential has yet to be realized because existing financing arrangements constrain its operation....The U.S. and Sault Ste. Marie results strongly suggest that we should be paying more attention to organizational models and payments methods other than fee-for-service.[5]

Interestingly enough, the creation of HMOs was one of the recommendations contained in the recent Gobeil report in Quebec.[6] The report indicated that such an initiative could reduce hospital admissions by 12 to 25 percent. Given the mounting costs of providing health services, it is only a matter of time before one or another of the provinces moves in this direction. Recently, both London Life and Aetna have moved into the area of providing dental maintenance organizations. If these turn out to be successful, they could well pave the way for HMOs.

## *Physician Supply and Paramedics*

Graham Scott, former Ontario Deputy Minister of Health, has argued that physicians must take a leadership role in any process of enhancing efficiency. To ensure efficiency, physicians will have to take steps to limit their own numbers. Should a substantial oversupply of physicians occur, physicians will require (generate!) more patient activity to maintain adequate demand for their services. Scott suggests that the proper alternative to increasing the supply of physicians is an increased use of paramedical personnel:

> By ensuring that our highest skilled and most broadly educated human resources within the health-care system are limited to an appropriate number, we can also minimize much of the debate and concern over the relative roles of the professions. Physicians will experience no pull to continue paramedical work and thus will better co-operate with and use paramedical resources. This change, in

---

[5]Stoddart, "Rationalizing the Health-Care System," pp. 21–22.
[6]Québec, Groupe de travail sur la révision des fonctions et des organisations gouvernementales (Gobeil report), *Rapport* (Québec: Editeur officiel, 1986).

turn, will partly shift the growth pattern away from the high-cost areas of medicine while it protects quality growth and produces more of the financial flexibility needed to support primary health care and illness-prevention programs.[7]

It is not clear that the incentives are such that an increased reliance on paramedics and nurse practitioners will come about naturally. The initiative will probably have to come from the provincial governments. Here again, Canada lags behind other jurisdictions, although there are encouraging signs. Saskatchewan's nurse practitioner program for primary school dental needs is a case in point. In Northern Canada, nurse practitioners are on the forefront of health care delivery. Denton et al. estimate that a full commitment to a nurse practitioner approach would produce savings in the neighborhood of $300 million per year.[8] Obviously, the ease of introduction of paramedics or nurse practitioners will depend on the reaction of physicians, which, as Scott has noted, likely will depend in turn on the supply of physicians.

It is rather a sad commentary on the health care system that recommendations for improving efficiency typically call for a reduction in the supply of doctors. For example, the Gobeil report actually recommended that one of Quebec's four medical schools be closed down. Economists generally argue that an increase in supply will be accommodated by falling prices. Unfortunately, under a fee for service system, in which the fees are set by government and the consumer is covered from dollar zero, the incentives go the other way. In the present context, cost cutting typically does imply reduction in the number of physicians. This state of affairs emphasizes the substantial incentive problems associated with a system based entirely on a solo practitioner, fee for service approach.

## Physician-Hospital Interaction

Under the present system, there is little incentive for physicians to make efficient use of hospitals. Indeed, the incentives are such that physicians quite appropriately view hospitals as a free, complementary input to their own delivery of health care. There are several possible remedies for this situation. I shall mention only one: a case can be made for placing all physicians who work virtually full time at a hospital on salary. As Alan Hay notes,

---

[7]Graham W.S. Scott, ''Comments,'' in Courchene, Conklin, and Cook, eds., *Ottawa and the Provinces*, vol. 2, p. 63.

[8]Frank T. Denton et al., ''Potential Savings from the Adoption of a Nurse Practitioner Technology in the Canadian Health Care System,'' *Socio-Economic Planning Sciences* 17 (1983): 199–209.

Physicians whose work is virtually all hospital-based should not be reimbursed on an open-ended, fee-for-service basis. We have suggested instead a negotiated salary, because it could eliminate the dilemma of the physician whose personal income [rises] from increasing, rather than limiting, the volume of services the hospital provides.[9]

## Alternatives to Hospitals

Alternatives to expensive hospital care probably represent the most promising strategies for reducing costs. No doubt all of the provinces are looking closely at convalescent homes, extended-care facilities, nursing homes, patient homes, and the balance between these and traditional hospitals. New Brunswick is one of the leaders here. Its Extra-Mural Hospital, which treats patients in their homes, is attracting national attention for its humanity, popularity, and economy. Provincial officials point to a daily patient cost of $21 compared with $300 in a regular hospital.[10] Moreover, by extending its use of this strategy, the province hopes to avoid the capital costs of building any new hospitals until the year 2000. Presumably, other provinces are undertaking similar experiments.

## Care for the Elderly

Canada's health care system is not efficient in its treatment of the elderly. Evidence abounds that existing institutions are not only overly expensive but often quite inappropriate for the needs of the elderly.[11] Given the present cost pressures on the system and the aging of the population, the provinces presumably will embark on a wide range of initiatives that will prove to be both more efficient and more appropriate.

## Consumer Involvement

There have been many suggestions for measures that would result in greater consumer involvement in the delivery of health care. Some of these measures call for greater reliance on user charges or financing techniques — fee per visit, extra billing, co-insurance, deductibles, and the like. The usual rationale for measures of this kind is twofold: to encourage efficient use of the health care system and to provide an additional source of finance for the system. Where measures of this kind have been put into practice, however, they have tended either to inhibit

[9]Alan Hay, "Is Ontario Paying Too Much?" *Hospital Administration in Canada* (May 1976), pp. 19–29.

[10]Caitlin Kelly, "New Brunswick's Extra-Mural Hospital provides independence, low-cost care," *Globe and Mail* (Toronto), September 30, 1985.

[11]H. John Gross and Cope W. Schwenger, *Health Care Costs for the Elderly in Ontario, 1976-2026* (Toronto: Ontario Economic Council, 1981).

access by lower-income groups or to run against the philosophical underpinnings of the Canadian system. Nonetheless, the provision of enhanced incentives at the consumer level is an approach that merits further attention, provided that the incentives can be made to agree with the equity concerns and the ideological basis of the existing system. Perhaps the best way to provide the appropriate incentives is by linking the health care system with the income tax system.

In 1976, the Ontario Economic Council proposed a cost-sharing scheme that would use the income tax system to relate a family's financial involvement in health care to both its use of services and its income:

> In Ontario, it would be quite feasible, with some adjustments to our current administrative and information system to establish a given family's use of the health care system, as well as a dollar measure of the benefits received. These benefits, subject to possible exemptions and castrophic limits, could be subjected to a form of income taxation. This whole process would be integrated with the income tax returns process in a manner such that the following conditions held:
> (a) taxation and hence financing of health care would be related to use and benefits received;
> (b) the poor would avoid paying because taxation can be geared to income, exemptions, and other ability-to-pay criteria;
> (c) ceilings would exist on the amount of taxation, thus building a castrophic insurance feature into the system;
> (d) averaging provisions would exist to permit a smoothing out of tax payments; and so on.
> Of course, whether such a system is desirable must be judged in terms of a number of factors including ease and cost of administration and how well it permits the achievement of the social and economic objectives of Ontario's health policies.[12]

Although this recommendation is a decade old, it was recently revived by Quebec's Gobeil report. The report argued that the first $2,000 of medical services in any year should be included as part of a family's taxable income. People with low incomes would pay little or nothing, but a taxpayer who now pays the top marginal tax in Quebec (27 percent) would see his or her taxes rise by $540 per year (that is, 27 percent of $2,000).[13] Since the tax would vary according to ability to pay, the Gobeil report does not view it as a "user fee."

On the surface, it would appear that a change of this nature would not

---

[12]Ontario Economic Council, *Issues and Alternatives, 1976* (Toronto, 1976), p. 15.
[13]Gobeil report, p. 44.

significantly influence the evolution of the health care system. In fact, just the opposite is likely to be true: the consumers of health care finally would play a meaningful role in the evolution of the health care system. For example, consumers would be able to choose between HMOs and solo practitioners for physician treatment — and if HMOs did not exist, consumers might well pressure governments to create them. They would also have the option of choosing between, say, extramural hospitals and regular hospitals or between hospitals and convalescent homes for institutional treatment. Moreover, governments could influence consumers' decisions by altering the financing available for these alternative approaches. Although all of this competition would take place within a "public" system, it nonetheless would generate efficiencies and allow Canadians a direct say in the evolution of the health system.

Many other areas of the health care system are also open to new initiatives. For example, Ontario and Alberta are experimenting with private-sector management of publicly funded hospitals (yet another of the recommendations of Quebec's Gobeil Committee). But the examples given above are sufficient to make the point that there are alternatives to the present system — some of them, doubtless, are more viable than others — that will appeal more and more to the provinces as they struggle to contain health care costs.

## *The Federal-Provincial Dimension*

At this point, the intergovernmental aspect of health care reenters the picture. There are two separate, though related, issues: the level of transfers from the federal government to the provinces and the conditions that are placed on the transfers.

In the 1982 renegotiations of the established programs, the federal government based its case for reducing the growth rate of its transfers to the provinces on the notion of "fiscal balance". Specifically, it argued that the provinces ought to shoulder more of the costs of the established programs, given the massive deficit at the federal level and the fact that the provinces had — at that time — an overall surplus. The Economic Council of Canada found this fiscal balance, or fiscal burden, argument wanting.[14] I would agree.

One can, however, mount an argument on fiscal discipline grounds to the effect that the level of government responsible for delivering a particular service should be the one that is largely responsible for raising the necessary revenues. As a matter of fact, the current system fulfills this goal at the margin, since each additional dollar spent by the provinces

---

[14]Economic Council of Canada, *Financing Confederation Today and Tomorrow* (Ottawa: Supply and Services Canada, 1982), pp. 6-9.

must come out of their own revenues. This outcome follows from the present unconditional nature of the transfers. If the federal government wants more provincial cost input, then it will have to provide the provinces with more tax room or be willing to put up with a rather dramatic acceleration by the provinces in their drive for economy and efficiency in health care. On the other hand, if the federal government has some preconceived views on how the health care system ought to operate across the provinces, it surely will have to pay to see this view realized.

My own opinion is that the needs, the technology, and the economic climate are changing so rapidly that the health care system cannot be forced to march in any one direction. This point leads to the issue of the conditions that are placed on the transfers. The thrust of the above argument has been that the provinces must be free to experiment. Efficiency is not the only consideration here: the appropriateness of certain aspects of the current system — its treatment of the elderly, for example — is also a matter for concern. It is in this context that the *Canada Health Act* reappears. In the view of Graham Scott — who, as provincial deputy minister of health, oversaw the evolution of the present system in Ontario — the *Canada Health Act* endorses the current structure of the health care delivery system: "It locks in all the 1960s' biases for more doctors and more institutions, and its emphasis suggests that the answers to our health-care problems lie in institutionalized, high-technology responses."[15]

My concern in this chapter is less with what the act does or does not do than with the future. Provincial governments must have the flexibility they need to innovate and experiment in the area of health care delivery. If they are denied the opportunity to increase the cost efficiency of health care, very serious consequences will follow for the whole range of other social programs, particularly given that both levels of government are operating under severe fiscal pressure.

Once again, it is important to make it clear that I am *not* talking about dismantling Canada's publicly funded health care system: all of the initiatives that I have discussed are fully consistent with a publicly funded health care delivery system. On the other hand, neither am I suggesting that any particular initiative be adopted by any given province, let alone by all of the provinces. This, too, would be to impose a preconceived structure on the system. What I am suggesting is that Canada is about to witness a veritable explosion of new approaches to health care delivery across the provinces. In Chapter 2, I argued in general terms that the pressures in the system of social programs are towards efficiency, decentralization, and private-sector participation. Nowhere is this likely to be more true than in the health care system. As for the federal government,

---

[15]Scott, "Comments," p. 59.

it obviously has a responsibility to ensure that all of this activity takes place within the framework of the accepted notions of equity, universality, and public funding that underlie the system.

Finally, there may well be considerable apprehension on the part of many Canadians if the provinces begin to "experiment" with alternative delivery mechanisms. Various provincial systems may become less uniform, at least for a time. It ought to be evident, however, that if one province finds a more efficient way of delivering a particular service, other provinces will follow its lead. We must not forget that it was Saskatchewan's experiments in the 1950s and early 1960s that gave Canada its present health care system. But that was a quarter of a century ago; the fiscal, economic, and sociodemographic challenges are entirely different now. Canadians must ensure that their health care system, along with all of the other social programs, meets these new challenges.

# 14

## Postsecondary Education

### The Challenges

Postsecondary education faces a set of challenges entirely different from those that confront the health care system. Unlike health care, which has been a "growth" industry since the change in the fiscal arrangements in 1977, postsecondary education is a "declining" industry: government funding for postsecondary education as a proportion of GNP declined to 1.24 percent in fiscal year 1984–85 from 1.35 percent in fiscal year 1977–78. Although the dollar value of this support increased by 1.5 percent in real terms over this period, this increase was swamped by the growth in enrollment in universities — 27 percent — and colleges — 36 percent. Thus, real expenditures per student in universities fell in every year between fiscal years 1977–78 and 1984–85.[1]

The postsecondary education sector differs from the health care sector in another important way. The federal government, through the exercise of its spending power, has been able to link the provincial health systems into a national system, with the result, for example, that there is full portability across provincial systems. Essentially, however, health care is delivered by the provinces. This is not true of postsecondary education: direct federal funding of university research, through the several federal granting councils, has long been an accepted part of the system. Moreover, the federal government's training (or retraining) programs have a very significant, if not direct, impact on the system of community colleges across the country.

Finally, postsecondary education is much more than a social program. Knowledge-intensive or human-capital industries will be critical to Canada's ability to compete in the future. This consideration makes postsecondary education, and in particular its research and technology transfer components, one of the cornerstones of industrial policy. In this sense also, this sector differs from health care.

This chapter focuses first on the role of the postsecondary education sector itself and then on the relevant federal-provincial financial relation-

---

[1]The figures in this paragraph are from A.W. Johnson, *Giving Greater Point and Purpose to the Federal Financing of Post-Secondary Education and Research in Canada* (Ottawa: Secretary of State, 1985), p. v.

ships, although it will not always be possible or desirable to maintain this separation of topics.

### Access, Quality, and Funding

The set of concerns facing most provincial governments in their approach to universities is the triad of access, quality, and funding. Unfortunately, these factors cannot be determined independently. If governments set goals for access and quality, then the funding level is by and large determined. Similarly, if funding levels are fixed and the system insists on maintaining existing quality, then access has to conform to these goals. The problem facing many provincial governments is that they have pared down funding while maintaining access, hoping that quality too will be maintained. It is likely that in all large bureaucracies, public or private, reductions in funding are consistent with maintaining both quality and access, up to a point. But the consensus is that in the case of postsecondary education, this point has long since been passed, with the result that the system is underfunded — probably seriously so.

How did the system get into this situation? I have already touched on one reason. Health care costs have mushroomed and the provinces have diverted funds from postsecondary education to health, in part because the constituency for health care carries far more weight in provincial politics than the constituency for postsecondary education. Second, the fact that the federal government was reducing the growth of established program transfers made it easier, politically, for the provincial governments to pass on some of these decreases to postsecondary education. Third, the prevailing opinion in the late 1970s (and perhaps later as well) was that the slowdown in birth rates would mean a reduction in university enrollments. Hence, a reduction in funding would be consistent with maintaining quality, since the number of students would be declining.

There are two reasons why these enrollment projections turned out to be way off base. First, although the size of the cohort reaching university age has indeed declined, this decline has been offset by the growing "participation rate" of the cohort — that is, the percentage of people in the age group attending postsecondary institutions. Some of this increase may have been recession-related, but the increasingly technological nature of society will ensure that the participation rate will increase gradually over time. Second, university education is appealing more and more to all age groups and not only to the young. In 1983–84, nearly 40 percent of Ontario university students (full-time and part-time) were over 24 years of age.[2] This combination of enhanced participation rates and the increas-

---

[2]See David K. Foot, "University Enrolments: Challenging Popular Misconceptions," in David W. Conklin and Thomas J. Courchene, eds., *Ontario Universities: Access, Operations and Funding* (Toronto: Ontario Economic Council, 1985), pp. 166–173.

ing importance of university education as an ongoing or lifetime activity has more than offset the decline in the size of the entering cohort.

A further reason for the current predicament of the university system is that provincial governments have tended to view the role of universities more in terms of social policy than in terms of economic policy: the objectives of social equity dominate those of economic development. Given this framework, it is hardly surprising that quality has been sacrificed for quantity. The conclusion to be drawn from this is not that the provinces should alter their approach to postsecondary education — although I shall make some recommendations along these lines — but, rather, that somewhere in the system there must be a greater emphasis on excellence and research. If the provinces cannot or will not provide this emphasis, then the task of providing it must be taken up by the federal government. I shall address this subject again later.

It appears that the prevailing view on the part of students, faculty, and the institutions themselves is that there is nothing inherently wrong with the system that a substantial input of additional government funding would not solve. Although the thrust of this chapter is that the system must move in the direction of striking a more appropriate balance between its social equity goal and its economic and industrial policy goal, it is highly unlikely that government funding will be forthcoming in amounts sufficient to achieve this new balance without substantial rethinking and reorientation of the existing parameters underlying the system.

I turn now to a discussion of three of the areas that merit such rethinking: tuition fees, the corporate-university linkage, and the national or "system" component of the postsecondary education sector.

## *Tuition Fees*[3]

The costs of instruction and associated research in Canada's universities and colleges are financed roughly as follows: 80 percent by governments; 14 percent by students through tuition fees; and 5 percent by other revenues available to postsecondary institutions.[4]

Given the reduced rate of growth of government transfers to postsecondary education, it is not surprising that there is a spirited debate on the issue of whether tuition fees should be increased. Arthur Smith, former chairman of the Economic Council of Canada, offers the following three arguments for a rise in tuition fees:

---

[3]This section closely resembles the section on tuition fees in Business Council on National Issues, *Social Policy Reform and the National Agenda* (Ottawa, 1986), which in turn reflects some contract work this author performed for the BCNI.

[4]Johnson, *Federal Financing of Post-Secondary Education and Research in Canada*, p. 9.

(1)...fees, as a proportion of university operating costs, appear to have fallen to approximately half the ratio of 15 years ago;...(2)...the average fee at an Ontario university has fallen even more rapidly as a ratio of average starting salaries of graduates (Waterloo cites a ratio of less than 5 percent); and (3)...these changes are implying a questionably high rate of intergenerational transfers from the taxpayers of today (with the bulk of all taxes coming from individuals with only modest to medium incomes) to potential high-income earners.[5]

Moreover, it is becoming more and more difficult to justify the large subsidies to university students when their counterparts who do not enter the postsecondary education system receive no such equivalent "gift" from the government. In addition, the job prospects are better for those who attend university than for those who do not. Indeed, equity considerations would appear to justify subsidies in the other direction. Davies and MacDonald, for example, suggest that both equity and efficiency call for a first-year subsidy for on-the-job training in place of the subsidy that the trainees would have received had they enrolled in a university or college.[6] An increase in tuition fees would reduce this inequity.

There is a further equity aspect to the issue of tuition fees. The argument for subsidizing education arises from the fact that there are returns to society as a whole from an educated citizenry — returns that are not fully captured by those being educated. However, the more that education embodies specific training or professional qualifications, the more likely it is that the individual will be able to internalize the benefits of that education, thereby lessening the case for a subsidy.

Yet the existing tuition arrangements stand this argument on its head. Given that tuition fees account for roughly 15 percent of the overall cost of education, it is likely that the portion of costs paid by the general arts student is closer to 30 percent, whereas the fees paid by an MBA or a law student represent a much smaller percentage, while dental and medical students pay a much lower percentage still. Precisely the opposite situation would be called for in terms of this externality argument.

To be sure, there are problems associated with raising tuition fees. A substantial hike in fees may risk financial elitism with respect to university access. As a society, we surely have reached the stage where it is unacceptable if otherwise qualified individuals are denied access to education because of their income status. What this observation implies is that any substantial increase in fees must be accompanied by an

---

[5]Arthur J.R. Smith, "Ontario Universities: Current Issues," in Conklin and Courchene, eds., *Ontario Universities*, pp. 414–415.

[6]J.B. Davies and G.M.T. MacDonald, *Information in the Labour Market: Job-Worker Matching and Its Implication for Education in Ontario* (Toronto: Ontario Economic Council, 1984).

expanded system of merit bursaries and probably by an expanded loan program based on a contingent repayment system — that is, a system where the paybacks are related to post-university incomes, up to some maximum.

In terms of the general issue of tuition levels, the following recommendations appear to be warranted:

• Tuition fees should rise to where they once again represent about 25 to 30 percent of university costs.
• The distribution of fee levels across broad programs should be adjusted to ensure that the proportion of costs covered by fees is roughly equal. What this implies, in practical terms, is substantially higher fees for programs such as dentistry and medicine, and for the professional programs generally, relative to the general programs.
• To ensure that income level does not become an important determinant of access, the rise in fees must be accompanied by an expanded bursary and loan program, with the latter preferably based on a contingent repayment system.

I have one other recommendation. Not everyone who qualifies for university or college is likely to be able or willing to achieve a university degree. But it is important that students not be deterred from finding out whether they are able or suited to pursue university training. Hence, the above recommendations for tuition increases would apply only *after* the first year. First-year fees, by design, would remain at the current 15 percent level in order to encourage students to experience the university environment. Should they then decide to go on, it would be appropriate and, indeed, equitable that they bear a larger percentage of the cost of their education than they would under the existing regime. Moreover, with one year already under their belts, the risk that they would be paying for something they do not want or cannot handle would clearly be minimized.

A regime of this kind would ameliorate some of the funding problems that currently beset universities and colleges. The case for higher fees, however, can be — and, indeed, my case here largely was — based on grounds of equity.

## The Corporate-University Interface

### The Traditional Approach

The corporate-university interface merits attention because it relates to the two issues singled out for attention in this analysis of the post-secondary education sector, namely, the funding of universities and the

## Table 21
### Collaboration between Corporate and
### Academic Institutes, by Type of Project

| Project | Purpose | Benefits |
| --- | --- | --- |
| Joint ventures Interface institutes Research contracts Research parks | Solving problems, creating and diffusing new knowledge | Expanding research capacity |
| University-based companies | Exploiting new knowledge | Commercializing university research |
| Cooperative education | Upgrading professional skills | Building personal linkages between faculty and corporate officers |
| Continuing education | | |
| Manpower transfer programs | | |

Source: Judith Maxwell, "The Corporate Relationship: Funding and Collaboration," in David W. Conklin and Thomas J. Courchene, eds., *Ontario Universities: Access, Operations and Funding* (Toronto: Ontario Economic Council, 1985), p. 284.

role of universities as a key component in Canada's industrial and economic future.

The traditional relationship between universities and the corporate sector is based on gifts and donations to fundraising ventures. Judith Maxwell, who now chairs the Economic Council of Canada, refers to these as "unconditional" donations, since very little intellectual interchange is involved between the donor and the university.[7] Maxwell estimates that in fiscal year 1982–83, Canadian universities received about $300 million in nongovernmental cash gifts, of which about half came from the corporate sector and half from individuals (alumni, for the most part) and foundations. Gifts and donations account for about 1 percent of total university revenues in Canada, whereas in the United States the comparable figure is 7 percent.[8]

The obvious question is why this sort of giving is so much more important in the United States. Part of the answer may be that Canadians view university funding as a responsibility of government. Part of it also may be that the tax systems of the two countries treat such donations differently. However, one obvious reason why Canadian universities obtain so little funding of this kind is that they make only lackluster efforts

[7]Judith Maxwell, "The Corporate Relationship: Funding and Collaboration," in Conklin and Courchene, eds., *Ontario Universities* pp. 279–280.
[8]Ibid., pp. 280–281.

to seek it out. The current financial squeeze on the postsecondary education sector ensures that universities will change their ways in this regard.

## The Emerging Approach

The new corporate-university interface is collaborative in nature, is based on intellectual interchange, and is motivated by self-interest on the part of both the university and the corporation.[9] Table 21 details the range of activities encompassed by this new relationship.

Why have these new relationships blossomed in the 1980s? Maxwell offers five reasons:

> First, global competition has forced the corporate community to hunt for new technologies, high quality graduates, and help in, for example, upgrading employee skills. Second, if you look at what the sources of economic growth are likely to be in this country over the next couple of decades, it's clear that we have to stop focusing simply on quantity, in terms of adding more manpower, more capital, etc., and turn our attention more to quality, in terms of upgrading technology and the human resources of today's workplace....
>
> On the university side, a third factor is the need for....funding, both for expansion and upgrading, and for what I call 'market knowledge', an awareness of what is going on in leading-edge industries. A sound 'market knowledge' ensures that universities set their research priorities and plan their curricula efficiently.
>
> A fourth factor pulling the two institutions together concerns the impact of technology itself. A number of issues here are relevant:
>
> — In many areas of research, there is only a short lag between the time of an innovation and the time that it takes to become a commercially viable product in the marketplace. Companies that are very aggressive in seeking out new product lines and services thus want to be as close to the laboratory bench as possible in order to be the first to bid when the proprietary rights become available.
>
> — There is an increasing need to combine disciplines, to bring together electrical engineers with mathematicians, for example, and any number of other skills in order to advance knowledge in key areas.
>
> — Regarding the higher cost of equipment, if you are going to have to lay out millions of dollars for a particular piece of equipment that is needed for teaching or for research on campus, it makes a lot of sense for corporations with similar interests to be available to contribute to the purchase of that equipment and also to have access to the use of it.

[9]Ibid., p. 283.

— There is a shortage of specially trained talent. The universities have trouble in hiring, for example, specialists in computers because they can't afford to pay the going market rate for them. One option for the universities and corporations is to jointly appoint such specialists.

A fifth factor that builds co-operative efforts is that some universities with international reputations appear to have corporations knocking down their doors in eagerness to participate in getting a particular piece of research done or with a desire to contribute to the teaching of a certain subject.[10]

Supporting these developments is the Corporate Higher Education Forum (CHEF), an organization of senior business executives and university presidents that was established three years ago in order to promote a stronger dialogue between the corporate and academic communities.

It is critically important, however, to recognize that with these developments comes a new set of challenges to the university community. The most important of these is the certainty that the corporate-university collaboration will focus on high-tech areas at the expense of the relative neglect of the arts and humanities. Thus, it will be left to the cooperating universities to cope with, or offset, the internal imbalance among disciplines that will result from linkages with the corporate sector. Second, the collaboration will surely alter some of the traditional values of universities — the freedom of information approach favored by universities will confront the closely guarded information approach that corporations favor in order to secure an advantage in the marketplace. In coping with these and other concerns, one of the first tasks that the CHEF ought to address is the establishment of acceptable guidelines and principles on which the emerging corporate-university interface ought to be based.

## *Postsecondary Education as a "System"*

The issue of the corporate-university interface provides a natural link between the concept of the university as an instrument of social and cultural policy and the concept of the university as an instrument of economic development policy. By considering postsecondary education as a "system", one that should involve interaction both between universities and colleges and among the provinces, this section will provide a further link to the later discussion of the "national" perspective with respect to higher education.

---

[10]Ibid., p. 285–286.

The first of these system concerns is the relationship between colleges — often referred to as community colleges — and universities. It is imperative that there be more of a two-way relationship between these two sets of institutions. Students should have the option of combining the education function of universities with the training function of colleges. It may not be possible to import to Canada the California system of transferability between colleges and universities, but the concept of enhanced interaction is surely valid. To date, the typical Canadian approach is to discourage such interaction and even to emphasize the "cultural" distinctions of the two sets of institutions. Yet a combination of courses, selected from both sets of institutions, may be far more appropriate for both the entry-age cohort and people engaged in mid-career retraining. One consequence of the prevailing insular approach is a duplication of facilities. Because colleges came on the scene relatively late in the game, many universities still offer technical courses that are more appropriate to colleges. Presumably, there are examples on the other side as well. From both a sociocultural and an economic vantage point, the familiar insular approach no longer serves either society or the individual client well.

The other system concern relates to the interprovincial dimension. Except perhaps in Ontario and Quebec, the notion that the various provincial systems can operate "independently" simply does not make sense — particularly when it comes to research activities and the development of centers of excellence. Given Canada's small population base, the various provincial university systems will have to "network" with each other if they are to generate the critical mass of scholars and funding needed to achieve excellence in many specialized fields. This is not to suggest that the record on this score is all bad. There is substantial mobility between provinces, especially at the graduate level, and the fact that there are no out-of-province tuition surcharges surely contributes to this mobility. The Canadian Institute for Advanced Research, under the presidency of Fraser Mustard, is an excellent recent example of an attempt to create a (nongeographical) center of excellence in the area of artificial intelligence by networking across several universities.

This trend must continue. If we build on our strengths, the system can be much more than the sum of its parts. This principle holds not only in the specialized areas, but extends to undergraduate education as well. For example, with the elimination of grade 13 in Ontario, there will be a once-and-for-all bulge in the province's university-age population. Surely it is not optimal for the Ontario system to gear up in order to absorb this temporary inflow on its own. I trust that Ontario officials are considering such initiatives as a program of traveling fellowships for study at universities in other provinces as alternatives to having its own system absorb the entire temporary influx.

## *The Federal-Provincial Overlap*

This brings me to one recurring theme of social policy — the interaction between the federal government and the provinces. In the context of postsecondary education, the intergovernmental issue is twofold: Is there a role for the federal government in this sector? What form should the large federal-provincial financial transfer take?

### *Centers of Excellence*

It is clear that there must be a "national" dimension to postsecondary education, by which I mean a dimension of the system that feeds into Canada's overall economic and industrial policy. For policies to be national, they need not be federal — that is, centralized — as Canada's experience with capital markets makes clear: there is little federal regulation of securities markets in this country, yet these markets have served Canada well. Nonetheless, it would appear that there is a role for the federal government in the postsecondary education sector.

A recent study by Al Johnson makes this point rather cogently. Despite the length of the relevant passage, it merits quotation:

> [N]o assessment of the financing of PSE [postsecondary education] would be complete without reflecting — indeed underscoring — the criticism that Canada, and Canada's governments and universities, have for too long been preoccupied with a determination to provide a good quality, near-universal, system of university and college education, and not enough with the aspiration to develop world-class centres of excellence within that system — centres which have earned or deserve an institutional, as well as financial, 'special status' within the system....
>
> To say this is not to overlook the significant specialization — and the excellence which flows from it — which *is* to be found in Canada's PSE system. Taken together, the universities themselves, through their heritage and their traditions, and through deliberate decision and imaginative innovation, *have* created and nourished some outstanding 'centres of excellence' (as they tend now, today, to be called). And Canada's granting councils, by supporting scholarship and research by the nation's best scholars, have tended to reinforce these centres of excellence — for the simple reason that the 'best' tend to gravitate to the 'best'.
>
> But it remains that the system, as such, is really not geared to support or to develop the kind of transcending excellence that one thinks of when one speaks of world-class centres: centres which set Canada apart, and which give it a lead; centres which are the 'one of a kind' endeavors that would be seen, by the public and private

university sectors alike, as being important to Canada's economic and technological and social development; centres which are of such breadth and such depth as to evoke the kind of institutional and budgetary 'special status' which they need.

Those who are knowledgeable about higher education have long known that there exist in the PSE system few incentives — whether for the universities or for most of the provinces — to create or to contribute to world-class centres (be they institutes, or faculties). For an individual university to do so is to undertake a venture whose costs would be financed at the expense of the basic educational function of the institution itself, but whose benefits would be enjoyed across the whole nation — and indeed beyond. Similarly, for a province to support world-class centres is to tax a constituency — the people of the province — which is much smaller than the constituency which would benefit from the centres — the whole of the nation (and more). This is not to say that no university, and no province — particularly the larger ones — has done, or would do so. They have. But it is to say that the fiscal and political incentives *do* work against individual universities and provinces creating and supporting world-class centres of excellence.

Only the Government of Canada, and for that matter the industries which span the whole nation, is, and are, in a position to finance centres of excellence at the expense of the same people who will benefit from them: the people of Canada. But even here, when speaking of the Government of Canada, the political pressures — which so often are more regional and provincial than they are national in character — tend to work against excellence, one has to be governed by where it is to be found, or where there is a base from which it might be developed, not by a desire to meet regional concerns. Equality and excellence, in short, do not always go hand in hand.[11]

What Johnson is saying, in essence, is that what the university system does well is to provide a high-quality service to Canadians, regardless of province. What it does not do well is to develop centers of excellence and research expertise, which, by their very nature, will not be allocated "equally" across the provinces. Moreover, he is concerned that even the federal government may not be able to accomplish this task. Hence, he recommends the appointment of a committee, composed of representatives of the universities, the private sector, foundations, and government, with a mandate to make the difficult judgments that are involved in choosing which areas of research or centers of excellence should be

---

[11]Johnson, *Federal Financing of Post-Secondary Education and Research in Canada*, pp. 30–31.

supported. Toward this end, Johnson recommends that some of the federal monies currently transferred to the provinces be earmarked to encourage the development of world-class centers of research and scholarship.

Certainly, the postsecondary education system should be encouraged to develop centers of excellence compatible with enhancing Canada's ability to compete in the knowledge-intensive industries that will characterize the world of the 1990s. The shortcomings in this area, however, are not limited to universities. Canadians appear to be experiencing considerable difficulty in making the transition from a resource-based culture to a research- or human-capital-based culture. University of Western Ontario President George Pedersen makes this point very effectively:

> The historical development of our economy, with its primary resource base, has provided little in the way of incentive to develop our research and development capacity. To put it in the extreme vernacular, 'if we don't cut it, or gut it, or dig it — we don't do it'.[12]

Canada has only a modest research-intensive industry base. As a result, there is less private-sector support for research and development here than in many other industrialized countries. The percentage of annual sales spent on R&D by industry has remained the same in Canada over the past few decades, in contrast to the substantial growth of this percentage in other western industrialized nations. This being the case,

> the creation of centres of excellence in research and scholarship may mean relatively little to Canada if we do not have industries that can exploit the knowledge base that is developed. To establish centres of excellence without addressing the R and D weakness in parts of Canadian industry would make it difficult for centres of excellence to contribute to maintaining and improving our position in the world.[13]

Obviously, the dimensions of this concern extend well beyond the parameters of the present study. Nonetheless, the point is a telling one. Canadians are constantly reminded by their leaders that from here on, Canada's most valuable resource will be its human capital. But an

---

[12]K. George Pedersen, "The Fourth Revolution: Which Side Are We On?" in A. Noordeh, ed., *Reforming the Financing Arrangements for Post Secondary Education in Canada* (Toronto: Ontario Economic Council, 1985), p. 30.

[13]J. Fraser Mustard, "A Discussion of the Centres of Excellence Proposal," in Noordeh, ed., *Reforming the Financing Arrangements for Post Secondary Education in Canada*, p. 53.

emphasis on human capital without the larger economic context to support it probably will also mean that human capital will be Canada's principal export. In my view, this larger context must embrace free trade and a willingness to challenge the world head on in the emerging growth industries. An emphasis on tariffs and protectionism amounts to maintaining an emphasis on the past generation's skills and human capital and serves only to erect barriers to Canada's transition from a resource-based to a human-capital-based culture.

To return to the issue at hand, the one proposal for enhancing research that appears to have widespread support is the recommendation that the granting councils reverse their stand against funding the overhead costs of research. In Mustard's view, paying the full cost of research, including overhead costs, is the "single step [which] would do more to help universities with the commitment to build centres of excellence than any other initiative."[14]

### The Funding Issue

The intergovernmental transfer arrangements for postsecondary education are currently in disarray. Not only is financing on anything but a permanent basis, thereby inhibiting system planning and stability, but the transfers themselves appear to have become part of a federal-provincial fiscal tug-of-war.

In commenting on this situation, the Macdonald Commission offered the following observations:

> [W]ith respect to post-secondary education, Commissioners believe that it is desirable to consider substantial changes in financing mechanisms in order to create a more competitive, dynamic and diversified system....[T]he [financing] should be changed to encourage reform of the system, but in a way that will minimize direct federal intervention in this area of provincial jurisdiction, while still allowing the achievement of national objectives.[15]

The Commission's goal was to remove the uncertainty associated with the current arrangements and to improve the incentives for institutions to achieve flexibility and excellence. It surveyed a broad range of alternatives for the federal-provincial component of postsecondary education funding. Those that it believed merited further attention included the following:

---

[14]Ibid., p. 59.

[15]Canada, Royal Commission on the Economic Union and Development Prospects for Canada (Macdonald Commission), *Summary of Conclusions and Recommendations* (Ottawa: Supply and Services Canada, 1985), p. 37.

— Replace intergovernmental transfers with direct-to-student transfers. Careful consideration should be given to the variant which makes much larger transfers to graduate students.
— Freeze current federal cash contributions. The federal government would...[then match further] provincial expenditure increases on a 50/50 basis.
— Freeze current federal cash contributions while redirecting considerable amounts (perhaps one-half) of what would have been the incremental amounts into funding of university-based research. The rest of the funds should be used to match, on a 25/75 federal-provincial basis, any increases in provincial government contributions to universities.[16]

The Commission's first choice was the direct-to-student transfers — that is, a ''voucher'' system. This, of course, would be a radical shift in approach. Note that the Commission's scheme would also provide larger grants for graduate students. This measure would contribute to the development of centers of excellence, since graduate students would be attracted to those universities perceived to be leaders in the relevant fields. Note also that an implicit condition of the scheme is that universities would have to increase their tuition fees in order to ''collect'' the vouchers.

Vouchers would have several other advantages. They would certainly increase the federal government's visibility in the postsecondary education arena, since they would be federal vouchers. They would also lead to enhanced flexibility of the system. Moreover, the universities would be put on notice that they would have to ''market'' their products to prospective students. British Columbia has an ongoing experiment with vouchers for primary education, and the Gobeil report recommended that Quebec follow suit.

Despite its potential advantage, the voucher system may not sit well with the provinces — although it would not appear to run afoul of the Constitution. By identifying it as its preferred solution, however, the Macdonald Commission effectively made the point that the present set of funding arrangements needs to be overhauled. This task may require considerable statemanship on the part of the federal and provincial governments, but the stakes are simply too high to allow the status quo to persist.

## Conclusion

It must seem anomalous that so much effort has been devoted to analyzing what, by any standards, appear to be very successful social programs. Canadians are justly proud of their health care system. And postsecond-

---

[16]Ibid., p. 38.

ary education particularly at the undergraduate level, compares exceedingly well with what the United States has in place. The issue is not what Canadians have accomplished to date, however, but whether these systems can meet the challenges that are facing them now.

For the health care sector, the fiscal-*cum*-economic challenge is to seek efficiencies in the delivery of health care that will slow the recent rapid escalation of health care costs. The related sociodemographic challenge is to have the system respond more appropriately to the needs of an aging population and in the process reap the efficiency gains that will result from a set of institutions and policies more suited to the elderly.

The fiscal challenge facing postsecondary education is that the sector, as it is currently constituted, is underfunded. The sociodemographic challenge is to embark on a rationalization that, on the one hand, will maintain appropriate access and, on the other, will make the system more responsive to the needs of the growing number of mature students and increase the interaction between universities and the colleges. The economic imperative is to ensure that the universities' sociocultural goals do not inhibit them from becoming a leading edge in the development of knowledge-based and research-intensive industries — a development that is certain to become an increasingly important component of Canada's overall industrial policy.

Both of these sectors face problems in the intergovernmental arena. In the health care sector, the federal-provincial overlap must allow the provinces enough flexibility to experiment with initiatives that may be both more cost efficient and more appropriate to the needs of users than existing approaches. For postsecondary education, the need is to provide greater stability in the intergovernmental financial arrangements while generating incentives that will foster centers of excellence. The problems of intergovernmental financing are complicated by the overhanging fiscal burden. It is likely that these challenges will have to be tackled within a framework of fewer, rather than more, total government dollars. Hence, federal-provincial confrontation probably cannot be avoided. Nonetheless, it is imperative for leaders at both levels of government to recognize that federal-provincial bargaining, important as it may be, must not stand in the way of a resolution of the issues appropriate to the needs of all Canadians.

The really fortunate thing in all this is that, in striving to ensure that health care and postsecondary education evolve in ways that are consistent with the underlying challenges, Canadians are starting from a position of strength.

# PART V

## The Equalization Subsystem

# 15

# *Equalization as the Overarching Social Policy*

## *Introduction*

The relationship between the federal and provincial governments in the social policy area is as pervasive as it is complex.[1] Indeed, the federal-provincial linkages, both financial and constitutional, stand at center-stage in all three of the social policy subsystems that I have described. It may promote a fuller appreciation of the complex nature of this interaction to note that Canadian social policy spans all three of the classical approaches to federalism — separation of powers, cooperative federalism, and checks and balances.[2] The separation of powers approach, or unilateralism, is reflected in the fact that the federal government has exclusive jurisdiction over UI, OAS, and GIS, while the provinces have exclusive jurisdiction over Workmen's Compensation, the QPP, and programs such as Ontario's GAINS. The obvious examples of cooperative federalism are CAP and the funding arrangements underpinning the established programs. Finally, the checks and balances approach is exemplified by the CPP, since neither level of government can change the system unless the other level concurs.[3]

The fact that all three classical approaches to federalism are effectively represented in the social policy arena suggests that it is probably of little use to attempt to address federal-provincial issues in terms of a single conceptual structure or framework. Indeed, it is probably more appropriate to view the federal-provincial interaction in the social policy area (and elsewhere) as one of process as much as one of structure or the division of powers. As Carl Friedrich noted,

---

[1]The analysis that follows is adopted from Thomas J. Courchene, *Economic Management and the Division of Power*, Collected Research Studies of the Royal Commission on the Economic Union and Development Prospects for Canada no. 67 (Toronto: University of Toronto Press, 1986), Chapter 6.

[2]See Keith Banting, "Federalism and Income Security: Historical Themes and Modern Variations," in Thomas J. Courchene, David W. Conklin, and Gail C.A. Cook, eds., *Ottawa and the Provinces: The Distribution of Money and Power*, vol. 1 (Toronto: Ontario Economic Council, 1985), pp. 253–276.

[3]The federal government has veto power over any proposed CPP changes, since Parliament must enact the legislation. Moreover, under the provisions of the legislation, any proposed amendment must be approved by two-thirds of the provinces with at least two-thirds of the population.

[F]ederalism should not be seen only as a static pattern or design, characterized by a particular and precisely fixed division of powers between government levels. Federalism is also and perhaps primarily the process of...adopting joint policies and making joint decisions on joint problems.[4]

In any event, the purpose of this chapter is not to rework or rethink the federal-provincial dimensions touched on in the previous chapters. Rather, it is to focus on Canada's system of equalization payments. The equalization program is, in effect, a GAI or an NIT for the provinces. As such, it is the overarching social program of the Canadian federation.

Initially introduced in 1957, the principle of equalization was enshrined in the *Constitution Act, 1982*. The act states:

Parliament and the government of Canada are committed to the principle of making equalization payments to ensure that provincial governments have sufficient revenues to provide reasonably comparable levels of public services at reasonably comparable levels of taxation.[5]

The following analysis outlines in skeleton form the manner in which the legislation converts these principles into practice; it also discusses some of the shortcomings of the current equalization program. To begin with, however, it is instructive to consider the role of equalization payments in the context of social policy.

## *Equalization and Social Policy*

Economists tend to assess the role of equalization payments in terms of equity, efficiency, or both. The equity argument is closely associated with what I have referred to elsewhere as the "nationhood rationale"[6] and it can probably still be expressed in much the same terms as it was expressed nearly a half-century ago:

In considering the relative fiscal needs of provincial governments, we are mainly concerned with a few divisions of their expenditures: on education, on social services, on development. It is of national interest that no provincial government should be unduly cramped in any of these respects. Education is basic to the quality of

---

[4]Carl Friedrich, *Trends of Federalism in Theory and Practice* (New York: Praeger, 1968), p. 7.

[5]Canada, *Constitution Act, 1982*, section 36(2).

[6]Thomas J. Courchene, *Equalization Payments: Past, Present and Future* (Toronto: Ontario Economic Council, 1984), p. 88.

disparities in the financial resources available for education should exist as between Canadian provinces. Social services, like education, cannot be subjected to marked disparities without serious reactions on the general welfare and on national unity.[7]

The efficiency rationale is somewhat more complicated. Because equalization payments reduce the tax price of public goods and services in the recipient provinces, they also serve to inhibit outmigration from these provinces. Of this there is little doubt, analytical or empirical. What is a matter of considerable doubt, however, are the resulting implications for economic efficiency. The traditional argument is that equalization runs counter to efficiency because it inhibits the natural adjustment forces: labor is less inclined to seek higher rewards elsewhere because of the subsidy for public-sector output provided by equalization.

A more recent argument is that equalization payments can enhance efficiency.[8] Essentially, the argument is that without equalization payments to the poorer provinces, there might be too much outmigration to some of the richer provinces. Consider, for example, the effects on migration of the energy rents in the western provinces. These rents accrue to provincial governments and are used to provide benefits to citizens. However, these benefits (or the rents that generate them) never enter citizens' incomes for tax purposes. Hence, even at identical market wage rates, persons may wish to move, say, to Alberta to "capture" some of these resource rents; this is "fiscally induced" migration. Equalization payments, in principle, could serve to offset this migration, since it is based on fiscal rather than on market criteria.

Neither of these rationales says much about the level of equalization. Indeed, some federations, including the United States, do not have equalization programs, which suggests that the efficiency argument is hardly conclusive. The United States, for example, likely would argue that differences in states' fiscal capacities are capitalized in the form of land rents and the like. Nonetheless, the equalization system has come to be an integral part of the way in which the Canadian federation operates.

There is, however, another rationale for equalization, one that may link it more directly to our analysis of social programs — the federal or constitutional rationale. If the provinces are to carry out the tasks assigned to them under the *Constitution Act, 1867*, they must have access to funds sufficient for this purpose. Equalization provides these funds. Moreover, if the provinces are to carry out their appointed tasks as they see fit, the

---

[7]Canada, Royal Commission on Dominion-Provincial Relations, *Report* (Ottawa: King's Printer, 1939), p. 80.
[8]See Robin Boadway and Frank Flatters, *Equalization in a Federal State: An Economic Analysis* (Ottawa: Economic Council of Canada, 1982).

equalization payments must be unconditional — as indeed they currently are.

In this context, it is particularly instructive to note that the equalization program was introduced when Canada began to transfer personal and corporate income tax points back to the provinces. The tax points were more valuable — in dollars per capita — in richer provinces than in poorer provinces; the equalization program was inaugurated to compensate for this. Because the ''rich'' provinces could spend the revenues from the transferred tax points in any manner that they wished (because they were, in fact, their own revenues), it became obvious that the compensating equalization payments should also be unconditional. In the Canadian context, therefore, equalization payments are not only the basis of a meaningful federalism — in that they give fiscal autonomy to the provinces — but also the instrument that sustains the present substantial decentralization of the taxing power. From this perspective, equalization is a program that affects all of the provinces, not just those that receive the payments.

The thrust of much of the analysis in the previous chapters was that the provinces should have the flexibility they require to design the various social programs under their jurisdiction in the manner most appropriate to their needs. And within this context, the federal government should concern itself largely with any national aspects of such programs. This point can be phrased somewhat differently: policies relating to ''place prosperity'' fall naturally in the provincial domain, while ''people prosperity'' — in the sense of overall labor market efficiency — is properly the concern of the federal government. It is with this framework in mind that I have recommended, for example, that the federal government ease its way out of the regional-extended-benefits aspects of unemployment insurance and replace them by national job creation programs that, during the transition, would be directed more toward the have-not regions. This framework is also the context for my suggestion that federal involvement in postsecondary education should be limited largely to the promotion of its national and economic policy aspects, particularly as they relate to research funding and the creation of centers of excellence. One of the principal policy instruments that permits such a conceptual and, one hopes, practical distinction is the system of equalization payments. In this important sense, the equalization program underlies the analytical framework adopted for this study.

However, this conclusion begs the question of whether the current equalization program is adequate to the task. To this question I now turn.

### *Equalization in Practice*

Table 22 presents data relating to the impact of equalization payments on provincial finances. It is evident that there is a wide variation in the per capita distribution of own-source revenues. In fiscal year 1981–82, for example, Prince Edward Island had just 55 percent of the national average level of revenues and roughly one-quarter of Alberta's per capita own-source revenues. The addition of equalization payments brought Prince Edward Island to 83 percent of the national average. If all federal transfers are included, this figure rises to 96 percent. Indeed, if one excludes Alberta from the comparison, the remaining provinces had access in fiscal year 1981–82 to overall per capita revenues ranging from 87 percent of the national average for Ontario to 106 percent for Saskatchewan. This is fairly convincing evidence that the system of equalization payments is achieving its stated objective — that is, through equalization, Canada has dramatically reduced differences in the fiscal capacity of the provinces to provide services for their citizens.

More recently, however, equalization has fallen on hard times. For over a decade before the 1982–87 fiscal arrangements, the equalization formula brought all provinces' revenues up to the national — that is, all-province — average. The only exception to this rule was that revenues from nonrenewable sources — essentially energy rents — were equalized only up to 50 percent of the national average. In 1982, the formula was altered quite radically. Revenues are now brought up to the level of five representative provinces — excluding Alberta and the Atlantic provinces. This arrangement dramatically reduces the impact of energy revenues on equalization, since Alberta is no longer in the equalization base. Moreover, because the formula downplays energy revenues, it also ensures that Ontario will not qualify as a have-not or recipient province.[9]

The new formula, however, has substantial problems. First, the move from the old to the new formula was facilitated by a series of transitional guarantees and minimum payment levels. As it turns out, most, if not all, of the recipient provinces' equalization payments are currently being determined by these transitional and minimum guarantees and not by the specifics of the formula itself. Under pressure from several provinces, in particular Manitoba, the federal government arbitrarily raised the guarantee levels in 1985, thereby moving the system even further away from being determined on the basis of a formula.

Second, because the Atlantic provinces are not included in the five-province tax base, any energy revenues that they receive from offshore oil or gas are subject to "taxation" at a rate of 100 percent; in other words, the offshore energy revenues, under the formula, should reduce equal-

---

[9]Although Ontario has never received equalization payments, it did qualify as a have-not province during the 1977–82 period. The 1982 redesign was motivated, in part at least, by a desire to ensure that Ontario would not end up as one of the recipient provinces. As the text indicates, the approach taken to ensure that this would be so was to downplay the role of energy rents in the formula.

Table 22

*Tax Base per capita, fiscal years 1972–73, 1976–77, and 1981–82*
*(national average = 100)*

| Measure of revenue base | Nfld. | P.E.I. | N.S. | N.B. | Que. | Ont. | Man. | Sask. | Alta. | B.C. |
|---|---|---|---|---|---|---|---|---|---|---|
| *Own-source revenues*[a] | | | | | | | | | | |
| 1972–73 | 62 | 59 | 72 | 71 | 85 | 110 | 90 | 85 | 134 | 120 |
| 1976–77 | 60 | 57 | 66 | 67 | 82 | 99 | 85 | 106 | 201 | 112 |
| 1981–82 | 59 | 55 | 66 | 66 | 78 | 94 | 79 | 112 | 217 | 111 |
| *Own-source revenues less natural resources* | | | | | | | | | | |
| 1972–73 | 61 | 62 | 75 | 72 | 87 | 115 | 93 | 82 | 111 | 114 |
| 1976–77 | 62 | 62 | 72 | 73 | 89 | 108 | 92 | 101 | 128 | 112 |
| 1981–82 | 62 | 62 | 73 | 73 | 87 | 104 | 87 | 103 | 139 | 114 |
| *Own-source revenues plus equalization* | | | | | | | | | | |
| 1972–73 | 85 | 84 | 87 | 87 | 90 | 104 | 93 | 94 | 125 | 113 |
| 1976–77 | 85 | 85 | 86 | 86 | 88 | 93 | 90 | 100 | 188 | 105 |
| 1981–82 | 83 | 83 | 84 | 84 | 86 | 88 | 88 | 105 | 203 | 104 |
| *Own-source revenues plus equalization* | | | | | | | | | | |
| 1972–73 | 95 | 102 | 91 | 92 | 95 | 101 | 95 | 93 | 121 | 106 |
| 1976–77 | 92 | 104 | 91 | 93 | 93 | 91 | 93 | 100 | 171 | 103 |
| 1981–82 | 90 | 96 | 89 | 92 | 90 | 87 | 90 | 106 | 186 | 102 |

[a] Own-source revenues and equalization payments are determined on the basis of the new equalization formula as far as tax bases are concerned. What this means is that all renewable energy resource revenues and all property taxes enter the equalization formula. The equalization standard, however, is the national average level and not the five-province average that characterizes the present formula.

Source: Thomas J. Courchene, *Equalization Payments: Past, Present and Future* (Toronto: Ontario Economic Council, 1984), p. 158.

ization dollar for dollar. Not surprisingly, therefore, the recent energy pacts between the federal government and Newfoundland and Nova Scotia include provisions for special equalization offset programs that allow the two provinces to pocket more of their offshore revenues than they would be allowed if the existing formula applied. In one sense, it is fully appropriate that there not be 100 percent taxation. But the real problem here is the neglect of the existing formula. The practice of divising separate equalization agreements moves equalization still further from a formula-based program and runs a real risk of undermining the broad support that equalization has hitherto enjoyed. Obviously, with the dramatic fall in world energy prices, the particular concern described here is now more one of principle than of practice.

The new formula has some other peculiar features. Because not all provinces are in the base, movements of industry, people, and capital across provinces can increase or decrease equalization depending on whether or not the origin and destination provinces are included in the five provinces that make up the standard.[10] These effects may not loom large in terms of dollar values, but they are indicative of the unfortunate conceptual problems that beset the current formula. For example, the effect on Quebec's equalization payments of a loss of a corporate headquarters should not depend on whether the corporation moves its head office to Toronto or Calgary. But this is precisely how the current formula works.

Thus, the equalization formula has become progressively more arbitrary during the 1982–87 period. Rather than being formula-based and widely accepted as an integral part of the federal-provincial interface, equalization is rapidly becoming the somewhat incoherent product of a series of one-on-one bargaining sessions as each recipient province seeks to enhance its own payment level. This process, taken to its extreme, could result in a situation in which the system of equalization payments is more a divisive than a unifying factor.

Hence, it would appear to be important that the equalization program return to its former status as a formula-determined system. In this connection, I agree with the Macdonald Commission's recommendations with respect to equalization:

- Canada should return to a representative tax system that includes all 10 provinces in the base. The present five-province calculation base allows too much room for distortion, strategic behaviour and unintended side-effects.
- Equalization payments should include some portion of resource revenues. There is no magic figure here, but the 20 to 30 percent range seems an appropriate compromise, since it approximates the

---

[10]For more detail, see Courchene, *Equalization Payments*, Part IV.

amounts that would accrue to provincial treasuries in the form of tax revenues if natural resources were in private hands.[11]

Even if there is general agreement to alter the formula along these lines, federal-provincial negotiations in this area inevitably will be difficult. This is the nature of the underlying fiscal challenge. The level of equalization provided likely will not be independent of actions taken on other fronts, such as welfare policy and established programs funding. Nor should it be. Nonetheless, the equalization system is such an essential ingredient of the overall social policy package and of the Canadian federation generally that special effort is warranted to ensure that it regains its status as one of the glues that bind Canadians together.

# PART VI

## Conclusion

# 16

## *Agenda for Reform*

Despite, or perhaps because of, the failure of the social policy review process that took place in the mid-1970s, social policy reform is once again on the nation's political agenda. In terms both of public awareness and of the "official" background documents, the process appears to be well launched.

Quebec's *White Paper on the Personal Income Tax and Transfer Systems*[1] draws attention to some of the serious efficiency and equity concerns associated with the transition from welfare to work and no doubt served as a catalyst for Ontario's recently announced comprehensive review of social policy. The Macdonald Commission's recommendations for a full-blown universal guaranteed annual income system as part of its overall reform proposals for the welfare work subsystem served to advance the concept of a "system" approach to reforming social policy.[2] The reports on unemployment insurance by the federal Forget Commission and the Newfoundland Royal Commission are now in the public domain.[3] In the area of postsecondary education, the recommendations of the Macdonald Commission and those of a report prepared for the Secretary of State for Canada[4] have alerted Canadians to the unsatisfactory nature of the current funding arrangements and to the need to integrate the sociocultural and industrial policy goals of higher education. More recently, the Quebec government has released special reports on privatization, deregulation, and the organization and management of government programs[5] — reports that contain rather dramatic proposals for the entire spectrum of social programs. To some extent, these Quebec reports

---

[1]Québec, Ministère des Finances, *White Paper on the Personal Tax and Transfer Systems* (Québec, 1984).

[2]Canada, Royal Commission on the Economic Union and Development Prospects for Canada, *Report*, vol. 2 (Ottawa: Supply and Services Canada, 1985).

[3]Canada, Commission of Inquiry on Unemployment Insurance, *Report* (Ottawa: Supply and Services, 1986); and Newfoundland, Royal Commission on Employment and Unemployment, *Building On Our Strengths* (St. John's: Queen's Printer, 1986).

[4]A.W. Johnson, *Giving Greater Point and Purpose to the Federal Financing of Post-Secondary Education and Research in Canada* (Ottawa: Secretary of State, 1985).

[5]Québec, Comité sur la privatisation, *De la révolution tranquille...à l'an deux mille* (Québec: Editeur officiel, 1986); Québec, Groupe de travail sur la déréglementation, *Réglementer moins et mieux, rapport final* (Québec: Editeur officiel, 1986); Québec, Groupe de travail sur la révision des fonctions et des organisations gouvernementales, *Rapport* (Québec: Editeur officiel, 1986).

follow in the wake of earlier federal studies published as part of the general review of governmental activities undertaken by the Nielsen Task Force.

Thus, a broad range of government-associated documents and a raft of others from special-interest groups and research agencies are providing an important backdrop to Finance Minister Michael Wilson's February 1986 budget announcement that the federal government is undertaking a comprehensive review of social programs in the federal domain.

If major reform in any policy area is difficult, it is particularly so in the social policy area, since social programs touch the lives of all Canadians. Inevitably, the reform process will produce winners and losers. Even with adequate phasing-in provisions and compensation for losers, reform will require a substantial degree of political will and commitment, since what is at stake is a reworking of major parts of the Canadian social fabric. Indeed, it is likely that meaningful reform will become possible only when Canadians as a whole come to believe that it is essential to their own economic and social well-being.

By itself, therefore, the fact that policy analysts can find fault with the existing network of social programs may not carry much weight. It would be surprising indeed if analysts could not suggest improvements in *all* programs at *all* levels of government. Hence, the relevant issue for social policy reform is whether Canadians deem the constellation of concerns highlighted in the previous chapters to be urgent enough to constitute an imperative for reform.

In general, one can imagine at least three distinct situations that could qualify as imperatives for reform:

• The original social policy goals are no longer valid; hence, some programs can and should be dismantled.
• The original goals remain every bit as valid as they ever were, but there are now alternative and preferable instruments available to achieve these goals.
• The original goals remain intact, but because of changing economic and sociodemographic factors, additional social policy goals now have to be integrated into the existing social policy framework.

I trust that it is accurate to claim that nothing in the previous chapters lends any credence whatever to the first of these three propositions. For example, the role of equalization has not been challenged. Nor has the publicly funded nature of the health care delivery system. Even the concerns over funding for fishermen and additional funding for have-not regions remain intact — although the thrust of the preceding analysis is that these objectives can be accomplished more effectively through policy instruments and delivery mechanisms other than the unemployment insurance program. Rather, the entire emphasis has been on the second and third propositions and on the manner in which the evolution of policy instruments, on the one hand, and the fiscal, economic, and sociodemographic challenges on the other, have combined to generate an agenda for reform. The following section summarizes the key aspects of this agenda.

## The Nature of the Agenda

Given the fiscal and economic cushion of the 1950s and 1960s, it was entirely natural that Canadians and their governments should have put in place a generous and comprehensive network of social programs. Moreover, if this buoyancy on the economic front still prevailed today (for example, if Canada was still perched at the top of the international rankings of GNP per capita), there would clearly be few pressures — let alone any agenda — for social policy reform.

But the underlying economic and social climate has undergone dramatic change. The world energy price roller coaster, the inflation-deflation cycle, and the worldwide recession of the early 1980s have ushered in a new era in the industrialized West. Industries everywhere are restructuring, and the new world trading environment is becoming more, not less, competitive. The rewards on the economic front will flow progressively to those countries that are able to reallocate resources in response to the changing patterns of world demand. Indeed, because of its small domestic market and the growing threat of protectionism across the world, Canada is under even greater economic adjustment pressure than are most of its trading partners.

The dramatically altered prospects on the economic front have equally dramatic implications for the role and design of social policy. On the one hand, social policy must facilitate and assist the occupational, industrial, and even geographical relocation that the new world economic order is requiring of the present generation of Canadians. We no longer have the luxury of designing social policy independently of the underlying economic environment. Specifically, we can no longer afford those aspects of the social policy network that impede adjustment or entrench the status quo: there is no economic security for Canadians in any economy that fails to adjust. On the other hand, this new economic order is also placing at risk entirely new groups of Canadians. Mid-career skill obsolescence was not of great concern in the 1950s and 1960s, but it is now emerging as a critical social and economic issue. As a matter of both social and economic policy, the social policy safety net must respond to these new challenges.

Thus, whereas the 1960s' cushion of sustained economic growth allowed Canada to develop a comprehensive social policy network, the message of the 1980s and beyond is one that calls for a rationalization of this network both in terms of reintegrating social and economic policy and in terms of reorienting the system to accommodate the altered needs of Canadians.

In more specific terms, the analysis in this study has focused on three underlying and interrelated challenges facing Canada's social policy architects. The first is the fiscal challenge. The deficit overhang at all levels of government and the competitive effects of the substantial income tax cuts in the United States severely constrain the ability of Canadian policymakers to maneuver on any expenditure front, social policy included. This constraint implies that any new initiatives are likely to come about only if existing programs elsewhere are pared back. Moreover, even in the absence of new initiatives, the pressure is on to find more efficient ways of delivering existing programs. Finally, as detailed in Chapter 2, a shift in the macro policy mix toward tighter fiscal and easier monetary policy is probably the most effective approach to economic stimulation.

The second challenge is the economic challenge. Essentially, the challenge here is, first, to ensure that the incentives within the social policy system work to encourage, rather than inhibit, the required adjustment and, second, to ensure that social policy evolves in a manner that reflects the changing needs of citizens in the adjustment process.

Finally, the sociodemographic challenge requires a reorientation of certain aspects of social policy to take account of new or emerging needs. The aging of the population implies that a greater proportion of social policy expenditures will have to be devoted to the elderly, a conclusion that, in turn, intensifies the concern that the relevant programs come under greater scrutiny to ensure that they are both appropriate and effective.

More to the point, the analysis has demonstrated that these challenges can all be satisfied. There is considerable scope within the existing fiscal parameters to effect substantial efficiency and incentive improvements in Canada's network of social policies and, at the same time, to devise alternative or new arrangements that are conducive to meeting the needs of Canadians. Hence, not only can challenges be satisfied but, as the analysis further attempts to demonstrate, they can be satisfied in a manner consistent with Canadians' views of equity. Moreover, the policy instruments most appropriate to the task of implementing these new directions already play an integral role in the delivery of the existing social programs. In a fundamental sense, then, the reform package is evolutionary, since it builds on policy instruments that are currently an accepted part of the social fabric.

The next section sketches the broad outline of the overall reform package.

## The Reform Agenda: A Brief Review

### The Retirement Income Subsystem

There is a general recognition that the aging of the population will make necessary a substantial increase in transfers of income to the elderly in the near future. What is not recognized so clearly is the fact that the income distribution of the elderly in the 1990s will be very different from that in the 1960s. The expansion over this period of tax-assisted pension plans and RRSPs implies that a very substantial segment of the next generation's elderly will be better off than are most current retirees. This being the case, the fiscal implications of the existing system, which provides roughly $6,500 in after-tax benefits *regardless* of income level, will become more serious. The thrust of the reform proposals is to place the upper-income elderly on a more comparable tax basis with nonelderly individuals or families with similar incomes. The net result of this enhanced targeting would be substantial savings, some of which presumably would be deployed to enrich the benefits available to the low-income elderly. All in all, the reform proposals clearly would meet the fiscal and socio-economic challenges, and they would also score high marks for increasing the progressivity of the benefits package for the elderly.

### The Welfare Work Subsystem

The proposed reforms in the welfare work subsystem are more far-reaching. First of all, unemployment insurance would be redesigned to place it more clearly on an insurance basis. The income support and regional development goals currently associated with the UI program would be hived off and incorporated in other programs and departments. The rationale here is straightforward: UI is a very inappropriate and ineffective instrument for delivering income support and job creation programs. On the welfare side, a major concern relating to efficiency and, more to the point, to the longer-term well-being of recipients is that the confiscatory tax rates associated with the transition from welfare to work generate poverty traps. Welfare recipients must have enhanced incentives to reenter the workplace and greater access to programs for retraining or skill enhancement. The freeing up of UI funds for job creation programs would help to address the latter concern, while enhanced targeting and an increased emphasis on refundable credits in the family benefits package of the income tax system would be a step toward addressing the former concern. The subsystem as a whole, then, would be moving gradually in the direction of an income-tested guaranteed annual income. Not only would the transition from welfare to work or from unemployment insurance to work no longer be subject to confiscatory tax rates, but the income-tested nature of the system would ensure that the working poor had relatively little incentive to resort to welfare. Moreover, the provinces would now find it easier to introduce corresponding incentives into their own welfare systems. Finally, the federal government, in the course of these changes, would assume a larger share of the responsibility for overall income support. This outcome, appropriate in its own right, would probably also mean that Ottawa would assume, proportionally, a larger share of the responsibility for income support in the poorer provinces — the very provinces that might experience some increased pressure on their welfare rolls as a result of the unemployment insurance reforms.

## The Established Programs Subsystem

The fiscal-*cum*-economic challenge in health care is to seek efficiencies in the delivery of health care that will slow the recent rapid escalation of health care costs. The related sociodemographic challenge is to have the system respond more appropriately to the needs of an aging population and, in the process, reap the efficiency gains that would result from a set of institutions and policies more suited to the elderly. The sociodemographic challenge in postsecondary education is to embark on a rationalization that would maintain appropriate access while reorienting the system so that it becomes more aware of the needs of the growing number of mature students and more open to interaction between universities and colleges. The economic imperative is to ensure that the sociocultural goals of the universities do not inhibit them from becoming a leading edge in the development of knowledge-based and research-intensive industries, a process that is sure to become an increasingly important component of Canada's overall industrial policy. Both of these sectors currently face problems in the intergovernmental arena. For health care, the federal-provincial overlap must allow the provinces enough flexibility to experiment with initiatives that may be both more cost efficient and more appropriate to the needs of users than existing programs. For postsecondary education, the need is to provide greater stability in the intergovernmental financial arrangements while generating incentives that will foster centers of excellence.

## The Equalization Subsystem

Canada's system of equalization payments is the overarching social program of the federation. In effect, it is a guaranteed annual income for the provinces. Recently, however, equalization payments to the poorer provinces have tended to be determined by ancillary features of the program or by bilateral agreements, rather than by the formula itself. The reform proposals consist mainly of endorsing existing recommendations — such as those of the Macdonald Commission and my own earlier recommendations — to return to a standard that includes all ten provinces and to bring, say, 25 percent of resource revenues into the formula — a percentage that is roughly the proportion of resource revenues that would accrue to provincial treasuries if natural resources were in the hands of the private sector.

## The Reform Window

The fact that the federal finance minister, in principle, has put most social programs and the tax system on the reform plate enhances considerably the prospects for meaningful reform. Some programs, by themselves, are quite amenable to reform. The family benefits package of the personal income tax system is probably the best example. Legislation that will extend the work of the 1978 reform in enhancing the role of refundable tax credits is already before Parliament — and it is possible, of course, to extend this work even further. However, although these changes will increase both the targeting and progressivity of benefits, they will do very little to achieve the efficiency and incentive goals of social policy reform. Indeed, unilateral movement on the family benefits front probably decreases the eventual likelihood of meaningful reform elsewhere in the system, since it means that family benefits reform can no longer be used as a sweetener to any overall reform package.

This is but a roundabout way of saying that although some components of the subsystem are amenable to unilateral reform, others are not. For example, it is much harder, both politically and economically, to contemplate substantial UI reform in isolation than in the context of a broader subsystem reform in which appropriate changes in other subsystem components, such as the family benefits package, could accommodate any negative spillovers and magnify potential incentive and efficiency gains.

With Ottawa's recent announcement that it is also pursuing tax reform, the window for reform has opened much further. There are at least two reasons why this is so. First, social policy and tax policy, particularly personal income taxation, are so closely integrated that much more is possible in the way of meaningful social policy reform if the underlying parameters of the tax system are also undergoing redesign. Second, by adding further instruments to the reform package tax reform makes it easier still to offset elsewhere in the overall package any undesirable consequences arising from changes in a given program. For example, any lowering of marginal tax rates — presumably the ultimate objective of tax reform — would help to ensure that the overall tax-back rates associated with the transition from either unemployment insurance or welfare to work fall well below their current confiscatory levels. Moreover, a shift in taxation from income to consumption — through a BTT — presumably would involve a refundable tax credit, an instrument that would move social policy some distance towards the long-term goal of a negative income tax. A refundable tax credit also would increase the federal contribution to welfare support in the poorer provinces, presumably an essential compensation ingredient in any reform designed to move unemployment insurance more in the direction of insurance principles.

To be sure, there may well be a trade-off here: at some point the sheer number of programs in the overall reform package may make it difficult to digest — even if the changes are of the incremental rather than the big bang variety. In my view, however, it is in this context of "global incrementalism" that meaningful reform is most likely to be achieved.

## Conclusion

There are grounds for optimism about social policy reform. The basic elements appear to be falling into place: the agenda exists, the reforms are eminently workable, both economically and politically, and the window of opportunity is wide open now that actions in the United States have forced a rethinking on the income tax front.

The analysis began with a personal note and perhaps it is fitting that it should also end with one. Analyses that, like this one, focus on social policy reform in terms of fiscal and economic imperatives are frequently very easy prey for staunch defenders of the status quo. Those who argue for policies that would enhance adjustment and longer-term efficiency partly at the expense of existing entitlements and short-term security can expect to encounter the charge that they are ignoring the deep-seated concerns of Canadians for compassion and equity. To put the matter differently, there is a temptation in many quarters to associate compassion and concern for one's fellow man with policies that embody entitlements and universality. Thus, those who espouse greater integration of social and economic concerns in the design of social policy are all too frequently accused of attempting to turn back the clock on Canada's hard-won gains on the postwar social policy front. I understand this view only too well, since it has dogged my policy writings for nearly two decades now. However, I obviously do not agree with it. Indeed, the motivation underlying this study is precisely to preserve these hard-won gains for future generations of Canadians. In my view, the real threat to our accomplishments on the social policy front, and the surest way to place these achievements in the balance, is to attempt to address the social and economic needs and challenges of the 1990s with a social policy framework that was designed specifically to address the needs and challenges of the 1960s.